2X

NORTHWEST
Inspirations
FLAVORS OF SOUTH PUGET SOUND

from the Junior League of Olympia

NORTHWEST *Inspirations*

FLAVORS OF SOUTH PUGET SOUND

Published by Junior League of Olympia
Copyright © 2009 by
Junior League of Olympia
108 State Avenue NW
Olympia, Washington 98501
360-357-6024

Cover Photo © by Doug Green
Unless otherwise noted, photography © by Doug Walker Photography
Food Styling: Dusty Huxford
Food Props: Drees
Wine Pairings: The Wine Loft, Olympia
Watercolor: *The Olympia Farmer's Market* © by Pete Bryan

This cookbook is a collection of our favorite recipes,
which are not necessarily original recipes.

Library of Congress Control Number: 2008925575
ISBN: 978-0-9799486-0-2

Edited, Designed and Produced by **Favorite Recipes® Press**
An imprint of

a wholly owned subsidiary of Southwestern/Great American, Inc.
P. O. Box 305142
Nashville Tennessee 37230
800-358-0560

Art Director: Steve Newman
Book Design: Sheri Ferguson
Project Editor: Tanis Westbrook

Manufactured in the United States of America
First Printing: 2009   7,500 copies

Contents

Introduction

The Junior League of Olympia's cookbook, *Northwest Inspirations*, was created to give you a taste of the diverse and fine ingredients of our region. This collection of recipes has been thoughtfully created and gathered from our community—the Olympia Junior League members, our friends, our families, and local chefs. These delicious recipes reveal the connection between the land, water, and seasons in the Northwest with the delectable local ingredients found in our unique area nestled between two mountain ranges, crisscrossed by rolling rivers, and edged by ever-changing ocean tides at the southernmost end of Puget Sound. These recipes will inspire you to prepare the finest of flavors from our region in your own home.

Our community gathers from April to December for the local bounty at the Olympia Farmer's Market. Rain or shine, friends and families gather here for coffee and tasty morsels, dance impromptu to the band of the day, and of course, to pick and purchase the finest local ingredients. While the Farmer's Market is one of the largest on the west coast, Olympia remains a small town where friends can run into each other over just-picked strawberries or freshly caught salmon. The Farmer's Market, a reflection of our distinctive community, is just one of the many reasons we consider it a privilege to live in Olympia.

The Junior League of Olympia serves an essential role in our community. We are committed to developing healthy families through numerous ongoing projects, and we create enduring friendships among our membership of women who are dedicated to making a difference in our community.

Proceeds from this book fund the Junior League of Olympia's mission and community projects focused on the prevention of child abuse and neglect.

Northwest Inspirations, *presented by Capitol City Honda*

THE OLYMPIA FARMER'S MARKET BY PETE BRYAN

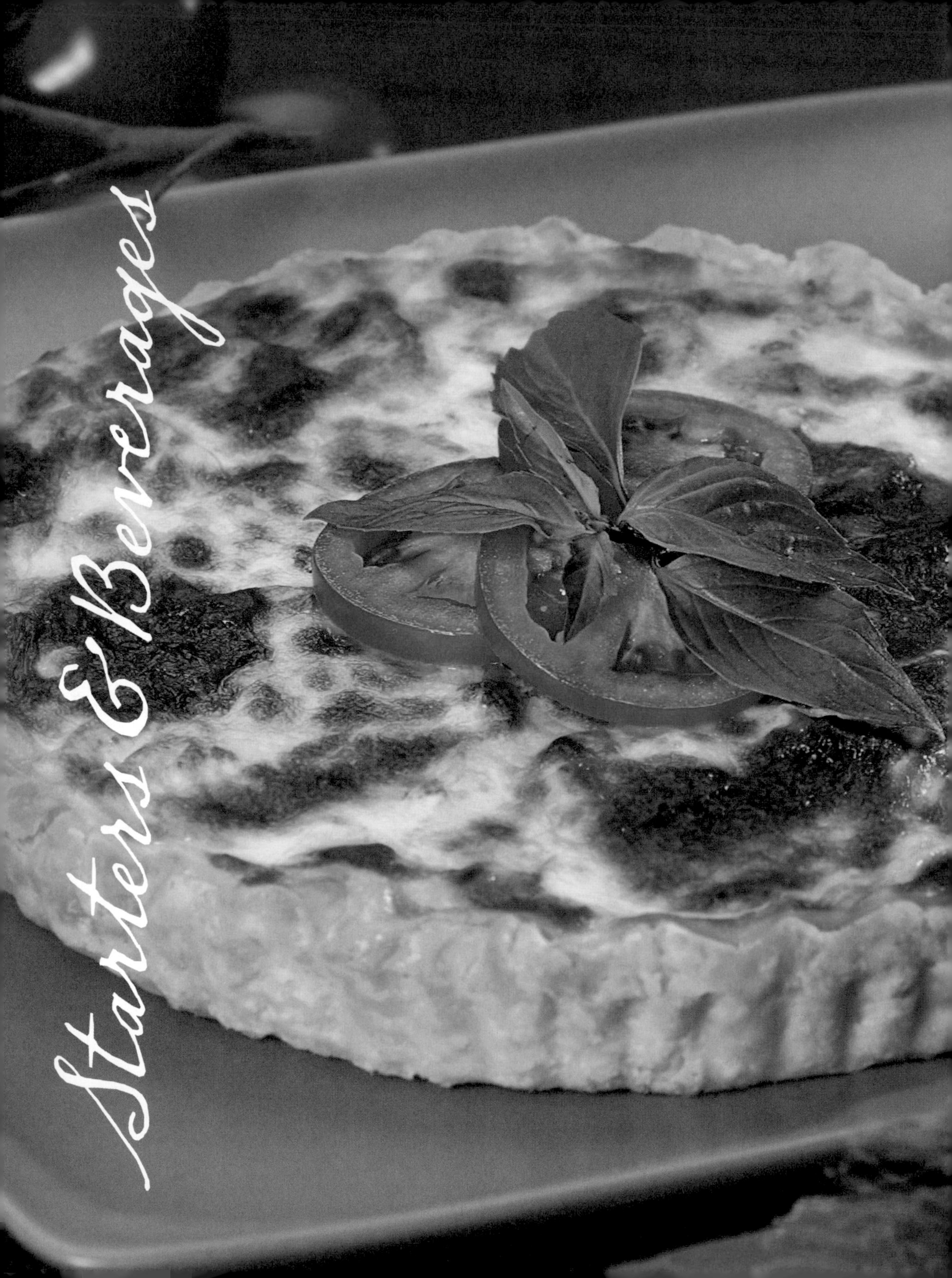

Starters & Beverages

STARTERS & BEVERAGES

◀ SUMMER TOMATO TART

Peanut
Chicken Satay

1/2 cup creamy peanut butter
1/4 cup milk
1 tablespoon rice vinegar
1 tablespoon soy sauce
1 tablespoon brown sugar

1 teaspoon minced garlic
4 large boneless skinless
    chicken breasts
Satay Dipping Sauce (below)

Combine the peanut butter, milk, rice vinegar, soy sauce and brown sugar in a bowl and mix well. Stir in the garlic. Cut the chicken into 1-inch strips and add to the marinade in the bowl. Marinate in the refrigerator for 1 to 2 hours. Soak eighteen wooden skewers in water.

Place an oven rack 4 inches from the heat source and preheat the broiler. Drain the chicken and skewers and thread the chicken lengthwise onto the skewers. Place the skewers in a broiler pan. Broil for 4 minutes on each side or until cooked through.

Arrange the skewers on a serving platter and garnish with cilantro sprigs. Serve with Satay Dipping Sauce.

SERVES 6

Satay
Dipping Sauce

1/4 cup rice vinegar
2 tablespoons sesame oil
2 tablespoons olive oil
1 tablespoon water
1 tablespoon brown sugar

1/3 cup finely chopped green
    onions
1/4 cup chopped fresh cilantro
2 teaspoons minced ginger

Combine the rice vinegar, sesame oil, olive oil, water and brown sugar in a bowl and mix well. Stir in the green onions, cilantro and ginger. Serve with Peanut Chicken Satay.

MAKES ABOUT 1 CUP

10 pounds chicken wings
1 (10-ounce) bottle buffalo wing
  hot sauce

2 dried red jalapeño chiles
3 tablespoons sugar
3 tablespoons rice wine vinegar

Combine the chicken and hot sauce in a bowl and mix to coat well. Marinate in the refrigerator for 2 hours.

Preheat a grill to medium-low heat. Drain the chicken, reserving the marinade. Combine the reserved marinade with the jalapeño chiles, sugar and rice wine vinegar in a small saucepan. Bring to a simmer.

Place the chicken on the grill and brush with the warm sauce. Grill for 20 minutes on each side or until cooked through, basting every 5 minutes with the sauce; adjust the heat of the grill as needed.

Arrange the chicken on a serving platter and garnish with coarsely chopped cilantro. Serve with blue cheese dressing for dipping.

SERVES 20

Caviar Pie

1 large lettuce leaf or several
  smaller lettuce leaves
8 ounces cream cheese,
  softened
1 small hard-cooked egg,
  chopped
1 tablespoon finely chopped
  shallot or onion

2 tablespoons mayonnaise
1/3 cup sour cream
1 ounce paddlefish caviar or
  other variety of caviar
4 lemon wedges
1 tablespoon capers
1 tablespoon chopped parsley

Place a large lettuce leaf on a small platter and spread with the cream cheese. Combine the egg, shallot and mayonnaise in a bowl and mix well. Spread evenly over the cream cheese. Spread the sour cream over the top and sprinkle with the caviar. Arrange the lemon wedges and capers around the edge and sprinkle with the parsley. Serve with crackers or toast points.

SERVES 8

Sweet Potato and Dungeness Crab Cakes

1/3 cup chopped red
    bell pepper
1/3 cup chopped celery
1/3 cup chopped onion
3 tablespoons unsalted butter
2 pounds sweet potatoes
1/2 teaspoon salt
8 cups water
1 cup panko bread crumbs
1/4 cup minced green onions
3 tablespoons chopped
    fresh parsley
1/4 cup mayonnaise
3 eggs

2 teaspoons Worcestershire
    sauce
2 teaspoons lemon juice
1 teaspoon Old Bay seasoning
1 teaspoon dry mustard
1/4 teaspoon Tabasco sauce
1/2 teaspoon salt
1/2 teaspoon pepper
3 cups Dungeness crab meat,
    pressed to remove moisture
2 cups panko bread crumbs
Olive oil
Chipotle Rémoulade (page 11)

Sauté the bell pepper, celery and onion in the butter in a sauté pan over medium-high heat until the onion is light brown.

Cook the sweet potatoes with 1/2 teaspoon salt in the water until tender; drain and let cool. Peel the sweet potatoes and then cut into small pieces.

Combine the sautéed vegetables and sweet potatoes with 1 cup bread crumbs, the green onions and parsley in a large bowl. Add the mayonnaise, eggs, Worcestershire sauce, lemon juice, Old Bay seasoning, dry mustard, Tabasco sauce, 1/2 teaspoon salt and the pepper; mix well. Mix in the crab meat. Shape into 3/4-ounce cakes and coat with 2 cups bread crumbs.

Preheat the oven to 450 degrees. Heat olive oil in a sauté pan and add the crab cakes; sauté until light golden brown. Remove to a baking sheet and bake for 15 minutes. Serve immediately with Chipotle Rémoulade.

SERVES 12

Chipotle Rémoulade

1/4 cup finely chopped green onions

2 tablespoons chopped fresh parsley

1 1/2 teaspoons minced garlic

2 tablespoons chipotle chiles in
    adobo sauce, finely chopped

1 tablespoon ketchup

1 1/2 teaspoons lemon juice

1 1/2 teaspoons Worcestershire sauce

1 1/2 teaspoons rice wine vinegar

1 1/2 teaspoons dry mustard

1/2 cup mayonnaise

Combine the green onions, parsley, garlic and chipotle chiles in a bowl and mix well. Stir in the ketchup, lemon juice, Worcestershire sauce, rice wine vinegar and dry mustard. Fold in the mayonnaise. Spoon into a serving bowl and serve with Sweet Potato and Dungeness Crab Cakes, or spoon a dollop of the rémoulade onto each cake to serve.

MAKES ABOUT 1 1/2 CUPS

11

Oysters Olympia

12 ounces Olympia beer or other regular beer
  (do not use light or dark beer)
12 fresh Pacific oysters in the whole shells
1 lemon, cut into wedges
3 tablespoons butter or garlic butter, melted (optional)

Bring the beer just to a simmer in a sauté pan. Place the oysters in the pan and cover. Steam for 10 minutes. Remove the oysters from the pan and discard the cooking liquid. Let the oysters cool for 10 minutes.

Pry the shells open gently and discard the smaller sides of the shells; reserve some of the oyster liquor with the oysters in the deeper sides of the shells. Drizzle with the lemon juice and butter.

SERVES 4

12

Reprinted with permission of *The Olympian/*
Steve Bloom

Olympia Oysters

Few foods evoke more passion among their fans than oysters. Oysters develop unique flavors and qualities depending upon the variety and where they grow. The tiny, coppery-flavored Olympia Oyster is the only oyster native to Puget Sound. The Pacific Northwest native oysters were nearly extinct due to overharvesting and pollution. The Olympia Native Oyster is now hand-harvested by a few family-run shellfish farms committed to restoring this oyster in its natural habitat. The Olympia Oyster is an excellent cocktail oyster, wonderful pan-fried or deep-fried. It is a distinctive world-class oyster.

Grilled Thai Basil Prawns

1/4 cup Thai basil leaves, chopped
1 teaspoon lime juice
1 tablespoon canola oil
1 teaspoon chile pepper flakes
1/4 teaspoon sea salt
24 prawns, peeled and deveined with tails intact
Phuket Lime Dipping Sauce (below)

Preheat a grill to medium. Soak eight bamboo skewers in warm water for 30 minutes or longer. Mix the basil, lime juice, canola oil, pepper flakes and sea salt in a bowl. Add the prawns and stir to coat evenly.

Drain the skewers and thread three prawns on each. Grill the prawns for 1 minute on each side or until pink and cooked through. Arrange on a serving platter and serve with Phuket Lime Dipping Sauce.

SERVES 8

Phuket Lime Dipping Sauce

10 garlic cloves
5 serranos or jalapeño chiles, chopped, or to taste
1 cilantro root
1 teaspoon salt
2 tablespoons sugar
2 tablespoons fish sauce
3 tablespoons lime juice

Place the garlic, chiles, cilantro root and salt in a mortar. Mash with a pestle until smooth. Add the sugar, fish sauce and lime juice and mash until the sugar dissolves completely and the sauce is smooth. Serve with Grilled Thai Basil Prawns.

MAKES ABOUT 1 CUP

Chef Pranee Khruasanit Halvorsen

Pranee Khruasanit Halvorsen, a Pacific Northwest chef and teacher of Thai cooking classes, loves to share food from her native Thailand. This is a well-known sauce from her home town of Phuket, where it is served as an accompaniment with grilled and steamed seafood, from crab, fish, and oysters to prawns.

Basil Garlic Shrimp

12 jumbo shrimp, peeled and deveined
Salt and pepper to taste
1 1/2 tablespoons olive oil
3 garlic cloves, minced
1/3 cup dry white wine
1 tablespoon fresh lemon juice
2 tablespoons chopped drained oil-pack
  sun-dried tomatoes
6 tablespoons unsalted butter, chopped
1/2 cup chopped fresh basil

Preheat the oven to 350 degrees. Season the shrimp with salt and pepper. Heat the olive oil in a large nonstick skillet over medium-high heat. Add the shrimp and sauté for 1 minute on each side. Remove to a baking dish using a slotted spoon; reserve the drippings in the skillet. Place the baking dish on the center oven rack. Bake for 5 minutes or just until cooked through.

Add the garlic to the drippings in the skillet and sauté over medium heat for 15 seconds. Add the wine, lemon juice and sun-dried tomatoes. Bring to a boil and cook until reduced by two-thirds, stirring constantly. Add the butter and basil and cook until the butter melts, stirring to mix well. Season with salt and pepper.

Place the shrimp in a serving bowl and spoon the sauce over the top. Serve with baguette slices.

SERVES 6

Smoky Cured Salmon

2 (1- to 1 1/2-pound) salmon
   fillets with skin
1 tablespoon Spanish smoked
   paprika (pimentón)
3 tablespoons sugar
3 tablespoons kosher salt

1 small red onion, thinly sliced
   and rinsed with cold water
3 tablespoons capers, rinsed
1 lemon, thinly sliced
1 cup sour cream or
   crème fraîche

Use needle-nose pliers to remove any bones from the salmon fillets. Place the fillets skin side down on a large sheet of plastic wrap. Mix the paprika, sugar and kosher salt together and sprinkle over the salmon. Place the two cut sides together and wrap with the plastic wrap. Place in a dish and arrange a plate on top. Weight the dish with a 1-pound weight, such as a package of coffee or sugar.

Marinate in the refrigerator for 4 days, turning the fillets every 12 hours, replacing the plastic wrap as needed and draining any liquid from the dish.

Rinse the salt mixture off the salmon and pat dry. Slice the salmon very thinly with a sharp knife, sliding the knife under the salmon to remove the skin. Wrap the salmon in plastic wrap and freeze for 10 minutes for greater ease of slicing, if necessary.

Arrange the salmon slices on a serving platter and add the onion, capers, lemon and sour cream. Serve with cocktail bread or crackers.

SERVES 15 TO 20

Spice It Up

This smoky salmon is so tender, it will melt in your mouth and amaze your guests. The sugar and kosher salt will "cook" the salmon by curing it. The smoked paprika, or pimentón, is the key to the flavor in this recipe. The peppers are smoked before they are dried and ground, giving the salmon a smoky and light peppery flavor, similar to that of cured lox. If you can't find pimentón, look for smoked paprika in the spice section of the market.

Arancine di Riso

1 cup leftover risotto,
   at room temperature
1 egg, beaten
1/4 cup (1 ounce) shredded
   Parmesan cheese
1/4 cup plain or seasoned dry
   bread crumbs

4 ounces fresh mozzarella
   cheese, cut into
   1/2-inch pieces
Plain or seasoned dry bread
   crumbs for coating
Vegetable oil for deep-frying
Salt to taste

Combine the risotto with the egg, Parmesan cheese and 1/4 cup bread crumbs in a bowl. Shape by rounded tablespoonfuls around the pieces of mozzarella, making twelve balls; larger balls will become too brown before the cheese in the center melts. Roll in bread crumbs to coat.

Heat vegetable oil to 350 degrees in a deep fryer or until a small portion of the rice mixture sizzles and browns evenly. Deep-fry the rice balls in batches for 2 to 3 minutes or until medium-brown, allowing the oil to return to 350 degrees between batches. Drain on paper towels and sprinkle with salt. Serve hot.

SERVES 6

Little Oranges

Arancine are known as "little oranges" in southern Italy and Sicily, where they are very popular street food. When the ferry arrives in Sicily from the tip of Italy's boot every morning, vendors are always there with fresh arancine wrapped in newspaper, much like England's fish and chips, to greet the visitors. For a flavorful base for arancine, sauté onions and garlic in butter to start and use equal parts wine and water to cook the arborio rice.

Brie and Gorgonzola Quesadillas with Pear Compote

8 flour tortillas
8 ounces Gorgonzola cheese, crumbled
8 ounces Brie cheese, cut into 1/4-inch pieces
Pear Compote (below)

Sprinkle the flour tortillas with the Gorgonzola cheese and Brie cheese. Fold the tortillas into halves to enclose the cheeses. Cook in a heated skillet over medium heat until light brown on both sides and the cheese melts. Cut into wedges and serve with Pear Compote.

SERVES 8

Pear Compote

1/2 cup (1 stick) butter
1/2 cup packed brown sugar
1/2 teaspoon cinnamon
4 Bartlett or Anjou pears, peeled and chopped
1/2 cup chopped walnuts
Pinch of salt
2 tablespoons cornstarch
2 tablespoons cold water

Melt the butter in a large saucepan over medium heat. Add the brown sugar and cinnamon and cook until the brown sugar begins to dissolve, stirring constantly. Add the pears, walnuts and salt, mixing to coat well. Cook until the pears just begin to soften.

Blend the cornstarch and water in a cup. Add to the pear mixture and cook until thickened, stirring constantly. Let cool to room temperature. Spoon into a serving bowl. Serve with Brie and Gorgonzola Quesadillas.

MAKES ABOUT 2 CUPS

Cheesy Stuffed Mushrooms

2 pounds button mushrooms
1/4 cup olive oil
2 teaspoons garlic salt
8 ounces cream cheese, softened
3/4 cup (3 ounces) finely grated Parmesan cheese
1/4 cup (1 ounce) finely shredded sharp Cheddar cheese
2 garlic cloves, minced

Preheat the oven to 300 degrees. Remove and discard the mushroom stems; wipe the mushroom caps with a dry paper towel. Place on a baking sheet; brush with the olive oil and sprinkle with the garlic salt.

Combine the cream cheese, Parmesan cheese, Cheddar cheese and garlic in a bowl and mix well. Spoon the mixture into the mushrooms caps.

Bake the mushrooms for 10 minutes. Place under the broiler and broil for 3 minutes to brown the tops. Serve immediately.

SERVES 6

18

Olympia Harbor Days

Olympia Harbor Days, held every Labor Day weekend, is a celebration of maritime history and tugboats in South Puget Sound. Working tugboats, as well as vintage and retired tugs, are moored at Percival Landing in downtown Olympia. The signature event of Olympia Harbor Days, the tugboat race, is one of the world's premier tugboat races. Tugs are built for power rather than speed, so when racing they create impressive wakes, which cause the boats to sway wildly from side to side as they race for the finish.

Spinach Artichoke Squares

1 (10-ounce) package frozen spinach, thawed
1 (13-ounce) jar marinated artichoke hearts
3 garlic cloves, minced
1 small onion, minced
1 cup (4 ounces) shredded Pepper Jack cheese
1/3 cup bread crumbs
2 eggs
1 tablespoon fresh parsley, minced
1/4 teaspoon dried oregano
Dash of cayenne pepper
Salt and black pepper to taste

Preheat the oven to 350 degrees. Drain the spinach and squeeze to remove the moisture. Sauté in a heated sauté pan over medium heat for 3 minutes. Remove to a bowl and let cool to room temperature. Drain the marinade from the artichokes and heat the marinade in the sauté pan. Add the garlic and onion and sauté until golden brown.

Squeeze the spinach to remove any excess moisture. Combine with the onion mixture, artichoke hearts, cheese, bread crumbs, eggs, parsley, oregano, cayenne pepper, salt and black pepper in a food processor. Process just until coarsely chopped and combined.

Spoon into a buttered 9×9-inch baking dish. Bake for 30 minutes. Cut into 1-inch squares and serve hot or cold.

SERVES 9

Blue Cheese-Stuffed Dates

12 Medjool dates
2 ounces good-quality blue cheese, cut into 24 pieces

Cut the dates into halves crosswise and remove the pits and any remaining stems. Place one piece of blue cheese inside each date half and insert a wooden pick. Arrange on a serving plate and serve at room temperature.

SERVES 6

Summer Tomato Tart

1 unbaked pie pastry
2/3 cup shredded whole-milk
   mozzarella cheese
4 Roma tomatoes, chopped
1 cup loosely packed fresh
   basil, chopped
2 garlic cloves, minced

1 cup (4 ounces) shredded
   whole-milk mozzarella
   cheese
1/4 cup (1 ounce) grated
   Parmesan cheese
1/2 cup mayonnaise
1 tablespoon milk

Preheat the oven to 425 degrees. Fit the pie pastry in a pie plate and then prick with a fork. Bake for 10 minutes or until light brown. Reduce the oven temperature to 375 degrees. Sprinkle 2/3 cup mozzarella cheese into the hot pie shell and let stand until the cheese melts.

Mix the tomatoes, basil and garlic in a bowl. Spoon into the pie shell. Combine 1 cup mozzarella cheese, the Parmesan cheese, mayonnaise and milk in a bowl and mix until smooth and spreadable. Dollop over the tomato mixture and spread evenly. Bake for 35 minutes or until the top is brown and bubbly.

SERVES 6 TO 8 AS AN APPETIZER OR 4 AS AN ENTRÉE

Inspired

Partnerships with other service organizations are valued in the Junior League of Olympia (JLO). We are committed to supporting local nonprofit organizations with their unplanned needs and expenses. The **JLO Community Assistance Fund** provides monetary grants to applicants who align with the JLO Mission, Vision, and Focus Area. We are inspired to touch our community through meeting these needs.

Fresh Vegetable Rolls with Sweet Chili Sauce

5 or 6 (6-inch) spring roll
   wrappers, rice paper
   wrappers, lettuce leaves or
   cabbage leaves
1/4 small jicama, shredded
1/2 large red or yellow bell
   pepper, julienned
1/4 English cucumber, sliced
1/2 carrot, shredded
2 ounces extra-firm tofu, sliced
2 tablespoons cilantro, chopped
2 tablespoons reserved sautéed
   garlic from the
   Sweet Chili Sauce (below)

Fill a large bowl with warm water. Place one spring roll wrapper in the water and let stand for 5 seconds. Remove to a plate. Sprinkle some each of the jicama, bell pepper, cucumber, carrot, tofu and cilantro on the lower third of the wrapper, leaving a 1-inch edge; the mixture should not be thicker than one inch. Sprinkle some of the sautéed garlic over the vegetables. Repeat with the remaining ingredients.

Bring the bottom edge of the wrapper up and over the vegetables. Tuck in the sides and roll to enclose the filling completely. Repeat with the remaining wrappers and vegetables. Cut the rolls into halves and arrange on a platter. Serve with Sweet Chili Sauce.

SERVES 10 TO 12

Sweet Chili Sauce

1 tablespoon canola oil
3 tablespoons chopped garlic
1/4 cup sweet chili sauce
2 tablespoons rice wine vinegar
1 teaspoon water
2 teaspoons chopped
   cilantro leaves

Heat the canola oil in a medium skillet over medium heat. Add the garlic and sauté until light golden brown. Combine the chili sauce, rice wine vinegar, water and cilantro in a small bowl and whisk to mix well. Add 1 tablespoon of the garlic along with some of the oil and mix well. Reserve the remaining garlic for the Fresh Vegetable Rolls. Spoon the sauce into a serving bowl and serve with the rolls.

MAKES ABOUT 1/2 CUP

Blue Cheese Ball

4 ounces blue cheese, crumbled
8 ounces cream cheese, softened
5 green onions, minced
3/4 cup chopped pecans

Combine the blue cheese and cream cheese in a medium bowl and mix until smooth. Add the green onions and 1/2 cup of the pecans; mix well. Shape into a ball in the bowl using a spatula. Roll the cheese ball in the remaining 1/4 cup pecans, coating well. Place on a serving plate and serve with crackers.

SERVES 10

Hot Artichoke Tapenade

2 (8-ounce cans) water-pack
artichoke hearts, drained
1 cup chopped tomato
1/2 cup fresh basil, chopped
2 garlic cloves, minced
1 bunch scallions, sliced

1/4 cup kalamata olives
1/2 cup seasoned bread crumbs
1/2 cup (2 ounces) shredded
Parmesan cheese
2 tablespoons olive oil

Preheat the oven to 400 degrees. Combine the artichoke hearts, tomato, basil, garlic, scallions and olives in a food processor. Pulse until minced and combined. Add the bread crumbs, Parmesan cheese and olive oil and pulse to mix well.

Spoon into a 9×9-inch or similar-size baking dish. Bake for 15 minutes or until the top is light brown. Serve with warm baguette slices.

SERVES 8

Spicy Crab Dip

3 ounces cream
   cheese, softened
1/2 cup mayonnaise
2 tablespoons Thai red chili
   sauce, such as Sriracha, or
   to taste
1 tablespoon fresh lemon juice

1 teaspoon prepared
   horseradish
1 cup fresh Dungeness crab
   meat, cooked
2 tablespoons minced
   green onions

Combine the cream cheese, mayonnaise, chili sauce, lemon juice and horseradish in a bowl and mix until smooth. Add the crab meat and green onions and mix gently. Spoon into a serving bowl and chill for 1 hour or longer. Serve with tortilla chips.

SERVES 4

23

Dungeness Crab

Dungeness crab is known around the world for its sweet, buttery, rich flavor. The crab was named after Dungeness, a small town on Washington's Olympic Peninsula. The oldest commercial shellfish fishery on the Pacific Coast began in Dungeness, Washington, in 1848. Today crabbing is both a recreational activity as well as a commercial venture. Crabs are commonly harvested with crab pots, but are also caught using ring nets or dip nets and by wading in shallow water during spring and early summer. Eating freshly cracked crab is a messy yet delectable Pacific Northwest tradition.

Reprinted with permission of *The Olympian/* Steven Herppich

Greek-Style Cheese Spread

8 ounces cream cheese, softened
1/3 cup minced or finely
   grated onion
1 garlic clove, minced

1 teaspoon sesame seeds
1 teaspoon dried thyme
1/4 teaspoon salt
1/2 teaspoon pepper

Combine the cream cheese, onion, garlic, sesame seeds and thyme in a bowl and mix well. Season with the salt and pepper. Shape into a mound or rectangle on a serving platter. Garnish with a sprinkle of additional thyme and sesame seeds. Serve with warm bread, crackers or cucumbers slices.

SERVES 4 OR 5

Cherry Cheese Spread

1 cup dried cherries
1 cup water
16 ounces cream
   cheese, softened

1 tablespoon fresh lemon juice
1/4 teaspoon grated lemon zest
1/4 teaspoon dried thyme

Combine the dried cherries and water in a small heavy saucepan. Simmer until the water is reduced to about 1 tablespoon. Remove from the heat to cool.

Combine the cream cheese, lemon juice, lemon zest and thyme in a medium bowl and mix well. Add the cooled cherry mixture. Spoon into a serving bowl.

SERVES 8

All-Day Spread

Serve versatile Cherry Cheese Spread any time of the day. Serve it with crackers for a quick, simple appetizer. For breakfast, spread it on scones or biscuits. Spread it on a turkey or ham sandwich for lunch. For dinner, cut a slit in the side of boneless chicken breasts or pork chops to make pockets and place a tablespoon of the spread inside before baking.

Pineapple Cream Cheese Spread

16 ounces cream
   cheese, softened
1 (8-ounce) can
   crushed pineapple
2 tablespoons chopped onion

$^1/_4$ cup chopped green
   bell pepper
1 cup chopped pecans
$^1/_2$ teaspoon seasoned salt

Combine the cream cheese and pineapple in a bowl and mix well. Mix in the onion, bell pepper, pecans and seasoned salt. Spoon into a serving dish or hollowed-out pineapple half and serve with crackers.

SERVES 8

Simple Smoked Salmon Spread

16 ounces regular or light cream
   cheese, softened
3 tablespoons milk

6 ounces smoked salmon or lox
2 green onions, minced

Combine the cream cheese and milk in a mixing bowl; mix with a hand mixer until smooth. Add the salmon and green onions and mix well; some bits of salmon and green onion will still be visible. Spoon into a serving bowl and garnish with capers and thin slices of red onion. Serve immediately or store in the refrigerator for up to 7 days. Serve with crackers or bagels.

You may also mix this in a food processor or stand mixer for a smoother spread. For variety, add a couple of tablespoons of the spread to scrambled eggs, spread it on wheat or rye toast, or stuff it into mushroom caps or hollowed-out cherry tomatoes.

SERVES 8

25

Tri-Color Torte

24 ounces cream
   cheese, softened
5 garlic cloves, minced
3 tablespoons milk
1 (6-ounce) can black olives,
   drained and finely chopped

1 (6-ounce) jar marinated
   artichokes, drained and
   finely chopped
1 (16-ounce) jar oil-pack sun-
   dried tomatoes, drained and
   finely chopped

Combine the cream cheese, garlic and milk in a bowl and mix until smooth. Line a glass bowl with plastic wrap and spread one-third of the cream cheese mixture firmly into the bowl. Layer half the olives, half the artichokes and half the sun-dried tomatoes over the cream cheese. Spread half the remaining cream cheese over the top. Repeat the vegetable layers. Spread the remaining cream cheese over the top and cover with plastic wrap.

Chill in the refrigerator for 1 to 24 hours. Remove the plastic wrap from the top and invert the torte onto a serving plate. Remove the plastic wrap and serve with crackers, pita chips or sliced French bread.

SERVES 8 TO 10

Thai Herbal Lemonade

1/3 cup sugar
1 cup water
3 stalks lemon grass, cut into
   halves lengthwise and
   crushed

9 kaffir lime leaves (optional)
2 serranos, cut into halves
1/4 teaspoon salt
Juice of 3 lemons
Juice of 1 lime

Bring the sugar and water to a boil in a small saucepan. Add the lemon grass, lime leaves and chiles and boil for 5 minutes, stirring to dissolve the sugar. Strain the syrup into a jar. Stir in the salt, lemon juice and lime juice.

Pour over ice in glasses to serve. Garnish with a slice of lime and a stalk of lemon grass for stirring.

MAKES 2 CUPS

Hot Mulled Cider

8 cups apple cider
2/3 cup packed brown sugar
2 cinnamon sticks

4 whole cloves
4 whole allspice

Combine the apple cider, brown sugar, cinnamon sticks, cloves and allspice in a large heavy saucepan. Bring to a simmer over medium-low heat and simmer for 30 minutes or longer. Remove the cinnamon sticks, cloves and allspice. Serve hot in cups.

MAKES 2 QUARTS

Northwest Mulled Wine

2 cinnamon sticks
4 whole allspice
12 whole cloves
Peel of 1 orange

1 (750-milliliter) bottle of
    Washington pinot noir
2 cups sweet vermouth
1/4 cup sugar

Combine the cinnamon sticks, allspice, cloves and orange peel in a large tea infuser or cheesecloth bag. Combine with the pinot noir, vermouth and sugar in a large saucepan. Bring almost to a simmer and heat for 30 minutes. Remove the spices and serve warm in 4-ounce punch cups.

SERVES 12

World-Renowned Washington Wine

Washington State is the nation's second-largest wine producer and is ranked among the world's top wine regions—remarkable considering it is such a relatively young wine industry. The opportunity to create distinctive, regionally unique wines has brought winemakers from all over the world. Pairings of Washington foods and wines are a delight for both chefs and connoisseurs. Washington has become highly acclaimed for its smooth, robust merlots and cabernet sauvignons, for its luscious, crisp chardonnays, and for its light, fresh sauvignon blancs and sémillons.

Coffee Nudge Punch

10 cups strong brewed
   coffee, chilled
1 cup milk
1 cup half-and-half
1/4 cup sugar
1 tablespoon vanilla extract

1/4 cup brandy
1/4 cup coffee liqueur
1/4 cup crème de cacao
1/2 gallon coffee ice cream
1 cup heavy whipping
   cream, whipped

Combine the coffee with the milk, half-and-half, sugar and vanilla in a large container. Add the brandy, coffee liqueur and crème de cacao. Chill in the refrigerator. Pour into a punch bowl at serving time and scoop in the ice cream. Dollop with the whipped cream. Garnish with a sprinkling of instant coffee granules. Serve in 4-ounce punch cups.

SERVES 30

Wake Up and Smell the Coffee

It's not unusual to see a coffee shop (or two) on every block in most Pacific Northwest communities. The coffee shop serves more than just your wake-up beverage. As you sip a traditional cup of brewed coffee or indulge in one of the many luxurious espresso drink offerings, you can enjoy music, commune with friends, take a break from the work day, or settle in to get some work done. Coffee is a mind-set, and we all need our fix!

Strawberry Champagne Punch

1 (1-liter) bottle lemon-lime soda, chilled
1 (750-milliliter) bottle white wine, chilled
1 (750-milliliter) bottle Champagne, chilled
12 ounces frozen whole strawberries

Combine the soda, white wine and Champagne in a punch bowl. Add the strawberries. Serve in punch cups. The frozen strawberries will keep the punch chilled as you serve.

SERVES 20

Spectacular Strawberries

Eating a Washington strawberry is an unforgettable experience. The berry is luscious, bursting with flavor, and distinctively red all the way through. Strawberries color Washington summers with their aromatic and vivid fields. The bountiful strawberry season peaks in June, when many Washingtonians can be found out berry picking. As their names suggest, Puget Beauty, Rainier, and Shuksan are quintessential Northwest strawberries found at local roadside stands and farmers' markets.

Reprinted with permission of The Olympian/ Toni Bailey

Brunch & Breads

BRUNCH & BREADS

◀ HAZELNUT FRENCH TOAST AND ORANGE ROLLS

Crab Cakes Benedict

1 egg
1/4 cup mayonnaise
1 tablespoon Dijon mustard
1 tablespoon Worcestershire sauce
1/4 teaspoon Tabasco sauce
1/4 cup minced fresh chives

1 pound crab meat
1 cup panko bread crumbs
1/4 cup canola oil
4 English muffins, split and lightly toasted
8 eggs, poached
Chive Hollandaise Sauce (below)

Beat the egg with the mayonnaise, Dijon mustard, Worcestershire sauce, Tabasco sauce and chives in a large bowl until combined. Add the crab meat and 1/3 cup of the bread crumbs; mix gently.

Shape the mixture into eight 3-inch crab cakes. Coat with the remaining 2/3 cup bread crumbs. Arrange on a baking sheet lined with waxed paper and cover with plastic wrap. Chill for 1 to 4 hours.

Sauté the crab cakes in batches in the heated canola oil in a large skillet over medium heat for 2 minutes on each side or until brown; drain.

Place two muffin halves on each serving plate. Top each with a crab cake and an egg. Drizzle each with 2 tablespoons Chive Hollandaise Sauce.

SERVES 4

Chive Hollandaise Sauce

6 egg yolks
2 tablespoons (or more) water
Salt and white pepper to taste

1 cup (2 sticks) butter, melted
3 tablespoons fresh lemon juice
3 tablespoons minced fresh chives

Process the egg yolks, water, salt and white pepper in a blender at high speed for 10 seconds. Add a mixture of the hot butter and lemon juice very gradually, processing constantly for 30 seconds longer or until thickened. Add hot water one teaspoon at a time if needed for the desired consistency. Stir in the chives just before serving.

If you are concerned about using raw egg yolks, use egg yolks pasteurized in their shells, which are sold at some specialty food stores, or use an equivalent amount of pasteurized egg substitute.

MAKES 1 3/4 CUPS

Twenty-Four–Hour Wine and Cheese Omelet

1 large loaf day-old French
  bread, torn into small pieces
6 tablespoons unsalted
  butter, melted
12 ounces domestic Swiss
  cheese, shredded
8 ounces Monterey Jack
  cheese, shredded
9 thin slices Genoa
  salami, chopped
16 eggs

3$1/4$ cups milk
$1/2$ cup dry white wine
1 tablespoon German mustard
4 large green onions, minced
$1/4$ teaspoon black pepper
$1/8$ teaspoon ground red pepper
1$1/2$ cups sour cream
$2/3$ to 1 cup freshly grated
    Parmesan cheese or
    shredded asiago cheese

Sprinkle the bread in two buttered shallow 9×13-inch (3-quart) baking dishes. Drizzle the butter over the bread. Sprinkle with the Swiss cheese, Monterey Jack cheese and salami.

Beat the eggs with the milk, wine, mustard, green onions, black pepper and red pepper in a bowl until foamy. Pour over the layers in the baking dishes. Cover with foil and chill for 8 to 24 hours.

Preheat the oven to 325 degrees. Let the chilled mixture stand at room temperature for 30 minutes. Bake, covered, for 1 hour or until set. Spread with the sour cream and sprinkle with Parmesan cheese. Bake, uncovered, for 10 minutes longer or until light brown and crusty.

SERVES 12

Cactus Quiche

1 cup chopped drained canned tender cactus (nopalitos)

2 cups (8 ounces) shredded Monterey Jack cheese

1 cup (4 ounces) shredded Cheddar cheese

1/2 cup chopped black olives

1/2 cup chopped Walla Walla onion

1/2 cup chopped seeded jalapeño chiles

1 cup chopped cooked pork chorizo

1 (9-inch) unbaked Chili Pie Shell (below)

3 eggs

1 1/2 cups heavy cream

Dash of cayenne pepper

Preheat the oven to 375 degrees. Sprinkle the cactus, Monterey Jack cheese, Cheddar cheese, olives, onion, chiles and sausage in the Chili Pie Shell.

Beat the eggs in a bowl. Add the cream and cayenne pepper and beat until smooth. Pour over the ingredients in the pie shell. Bake for 45 minutes. Cut into wedges and serve with salsa, if desired.

SERVES 6

Chili Pie Shell

2 cups all-purpose flour

1 tablespoon chili powder

1 teaspoon salt

2/3 cup shortening

4 to 5 tablespoons cold water

Combine the flour, chili powder and salt in a bowl. Cut in the shortening until crumbly. Add enough water to form a dough and shape into a ball. Roll into a circle on a lightly floured surface and fit into a 9-inch pie plate; trim to fit.

MAKES 1 PIE SHELL

Quiche Quickly

3 eggs
1¹/4 cups milk
1 tablespoon butter, melted
¹/2 cup all-purpose flour
¹/2 teaspoon baking powder
¹/4 teaspoon salt
¹/8 teaspoon black pepper
¹/8 teaspoon cayenne pepper

2 (8-ounce) cans smoked
   salmon, drained
1 cup (4 ounces) shredded
   sharp Cheddar cheese
1 cup chopped
   Walla Walla onion
1 unbaked (9-inch) pie shell

Preheat the oven to 300 degrees. Combine the eggs, milk, butter, flour, baking powder, salt, black pepper and cayenne pepper in a food processor and process until smooth. Combine with the salmon, Cheddar cheese and onion in a bowl and mix well.

Spoon the salmon mixture into the pie shell. Bake for 45 minutes. Serve immediately or store in the refrigerator to reheat and serve the next day.

SERVES 6

Inspiring

Kids in the Kitchen is all about future cooks and inspiring good eating habits. Junior Leagues across the country have teamed up to address the urgent issues surrounding childhood obesity and poor nutrition. Locally, the Junior League of Olympia offers educational, fun-filled events that help children learn about healthful foods and their bodies.

Eggs Benedict Strata

6 English muffins, split
8 ounces fresh asparagus, trimmed and cut into 1-inch pieces
4 hard-cooked eggs, chopped
6 ounces Canadian bacon, coarsely chopped
1 cup (4 ounces) shredded Swiss cheese
Salt and freshly ground black pepper to taste
2/3 cup chicken broth
2 eggs
1/2 cup fresh lemon juice
1 egg
1 cup heavy cream
1 cup milk
Cayenne pepper to taste
1 tablespoon butter, softened

Let the English muffins stand at room temperature for 12 hours to dry or dry in a 250-degree oven for 1 hour. Arrange the muffin bottoms cut sides up in a single layer in a buttered 9×13-inch baking pan.

Cook the asparagus in boiling water in a saucepan for 4 minutes or just until tender. Drain in a colander, rinse and drain well again.

Sprinkle the hard-cooked eggs, Canadian bacon, asparagus, Swiss cheese, salt and black pepper over the English muffins.

Bring the chicken broth to a boil in a small saucepan. Whisk two eggs with the lemon juice in a bowl. Whisk half the broth into the egg mixture, then whisk the egg mixture into the broth. Cook over medium-low heat until thickened; do not allow to boil.

Whisk one egg with the cream, milk and cayenne pepper in a bowl. Add the hot mixture gradually, whisking constantly until combined. Pour evenly over the muffins in the baking dish.

Spread the butter over the cut sides of the muffin tops and place in a food processor; pulse until crumbly. Sprinkle evenly over the strata. Cover with foil and chill for 1 to 12 hours; a longer chilling time will yield a more custard-like consistency.

Preheat the oven to 350 degrees. Bake the strata, uncovered, for 35 to 45 minutes or until set. You may substitute fresh broccoli for the asparagus.

SERVES 6 TO 8

Roma Spinach Strata

1 small onion, chopped
4 garlic cloves, minced
8 ounces mushrooms,
   thinly sliced
Pinch of red pepper flakes
2 tablespoons butter
2 tablespoons all-purpose flour
1 pound fresh baby spinach
1/2 teaspoon salt
1/2 teaspoon freshly ground
   black pepper
1 (16-ounce) baguette French
   bread, cut into 1-inch slices
5 Roma tomatoes, thinly sliced

1/2 cup crumbled feta cheese
1/2 cup (2 ounces) grated
   Romano cheese
8 eggs
11/2 cups milk
11/2 cups half-and-half
2 tablespoons Dijon mustard
2 teaspoons oregano
1/2 teaspoon salt
1/4 teaspoon freshly ground
   black pepper
1/2 cup (2 ounces) grated
   Romano cheese

Sauté the onion, garlic, mushrooms and red pepper flakes in the butter in a large skillet over medium-high heat until the vegetables are tender. Sprinkle with the flour and cook for 1 minute, stirring to mix well. Add half the spinach at a time and cook until wilted after each addition, stirring constantly. Remove from the heat and season with 1/2 teaspoon salt and 1/2 teaspoon black pepper.

Arrange half the baguette slices in a single layer in a 9×13-inch baking dish lightly coated with olive oil. Layer the spinach mixture and tomato slices over the bread. Sprinkle with the feta cheese and 1/2 cup Romano cheese. Top with the remaining baguette slices.

Beat the eggs in a large bowl. Add the milk, half-and-half, Dijon mustard, oregano, 1/2 teaspoon salt and 1/4 teaspoon black pepper; mix well. Pour over the strata and sprinkle with 1/2 cup Romano cheese. Cover tightly with foil and chill for 8 to 12 hours.

Preheat the oven to 350 minutes. Bake the strata, uncovered, for 35 to 40 minutes or until set. Serve with sliced ham or grilled Italian sausage.

SERVES 6 TO 8

Reuben-on-Rye Brunch Pie

1 cup sauerkraut, rinsed and drained
1 loaf rye bread, sliced and crusts trimmed
1 tablespoon German stone-ground mustard
3 ounces pastrami or corned beef, thinly sliced
1 cup (4 ounces) shredded or chopped Muenster cheese

1/4 cup minced onion
4 eggs
1 cup half-and-half
1 teaspoon caraway seeds
1 teaspoon garlic powder
1 teaspoon salt
1/2 teaspoon pepper
2 tablespoons shredded Parmesan cheese

Preheat the oven to 425 degrees. Pat the sauerkraut dry with paper towels. Arrange the bread over the bottom and side of a buttered pie plate or quiche pan, trimming the bread to fit where necessary. Spread the mustard over the bread. Layer the pastrami, Muenster cheese, sauerkraut and onion over the bread.

Combine the eggs, half-and-half, caraway seeds, garlic powder, salt and pepper in a bowl and beat until smooth. Pour carefully over the layers. Sprinkle with the Parmesan cheese.

Place on a baking sheet and bake for 15 minutes. Reduce the heat to 300 degrees and bake for 30 minutes longer or until a knife inserted in the center comes out clean.

SERVES 6

Baked Brunch Sandwiches

2 (12-count) packages Hawaiian sweet rolls
1 pound deli ham, sliced
16 ounces Swiss cheese, sliced
3/4 cup (1 1/2 sticks) butter, melted
2 tablespoons Dijon mustard
1 tablespoon Worcestershire sauce
2 tablespoons minced Walla Walla onion
1 teaspoon poppy seeds

Split the entire packages of sweet rolls horizontally. Place the bottom portions of the rolls in a 9×13-inch baking pan. Layer the ham and cheese over the rolls and replace the top portions of the rolls.

Combine the butter, Dijon mustard, Worcestershire sauce, onion and poppy seeds in a bowl and mix well. Drizzle the mixture over the rolls. Cover with foil and chill for 8 hours or longer.

Preheat the oven to 350 degrees. Bake the sandwiches for 15 minutes or until golden brown. Cut the rolls apart and serve.

SERVES 12

Breakfast Sandwich Italiano

1 slice panini bread
1 egg, beaten
1/2 cup water
1/4 cup (1 ounce) shredded
 provolone cheese
1 slice prosciutto
1/4 cup fresh baby spinach
3 leaves fresh basil

1/2 lemon
1 slice provolone cheese
1/4 cup chopped
 Walla Walla onion
3 Roma tomatoes, thinly sliced
Kosher salt and cracked pepper
 to taste

Preheat the broiler. Cut the bread into halves and broil just until warm but not crisp. Pour the egg into a heated omelet pan and add the water. Poach the egg for 2 minutes.

Place one portion of the bread on a baking sheet and layer the shredded provolone cheese, prosciutto, spinach and basil in the order listed on the bread. Squeeze the juice of the lemon over the basil. Layer the slice of provolone cheese, onion and tomatoes over the basil and sprinkle with kosher salt and cracked pepper.

Broil the open sandwich just until the sliced cheese melts. Drain the egg and then fold in half. Place the egg on the sandwich and top with the remaining bread. Brush with olive oil and serve.

SERVES 1

Apple Cranberry-Baked Bacon

1 pound thick-cut deli bacon
1/8 teaspoon cayenne pepper
1/4 cup Apple Cranberry Chutney (below)

Preheat the oven to 350 degrees. Place a wire rack on a baking sheet with sides. Arrange the bacon on the rack with the sides not touching. Bake for 15 minutes.

Process the cayenne pepper and Apple Cranberry Chutney in a food processor until smooth. Brush over the bacon. Bake for 5 minutes longer, watching carefully to prevent overbrowning.

SERVES 8

Apple Cranberry Chutney

1 apple, peeled, cored and chopped
1 cup whole fresh or frozen cranberries
1/2 cup water
1/4 cup sugar
1 teaspoon grated fresh ginger
1 teaspoon grated orange zest
1 teaspoon cinnamon

Combine the apple, cranberries, water, sugar, ginger, orange zest and cinnamon in a saucepan and mix well. Cook over medium-low heat until the apple and cranberries are tender. Cool to room temperature.

MAKES 2 1/2 CUPS

Cinnamon Bread Pudding

3 cups (1-inch pieces) cinnamon rolls or Danish rolls
2 cups cream, milk or half-and-half

1 tablespoon vanilla extract
1/4 cup sugar
4 eggs
1/4 cup sugar

Preheat the oven to 350 degrees. Spread the bread in a 10-inch springform pan.

Combine the cream, vanilla and 1/4 cup sugar in a saucepan. Bring just to a simmer; do not boil. Beat the eggs with 1/4 cup sugar in a bowl until smooth. Add the hot milk very gradually to the eggs, whisking constantly until the mixture is smooth and the sugar dissolves. Pour over the rolls and let stand for 15 minutes.

Cover the springform pan with plastic wrap and then foil. Place the springform pan in a larger baking dish and add water to the dish. Bake for 45 minutes or until the center reaches 160 degrees on a thermometer. Reduce the oven temperature to 275 degrees and bake for 10 minutes longer. Cool to room temperature.

SERVES 8

42

Reprinted with permission of *The Olympian/* Tony Overman

Capital Lakefair Festival

Lakefair is one of Washington's largest community festivals. This five-day summer extravaganza draws families from throughout South Puget Sound to a fun-filled carnival, the crowning of the Lakefair Queen, and the Grand Twilight Parade, featuring floats from around the state. The sports-minded enjoy the powerboat races, the outdoor volleyball tournament on the Capitol campus, and the Lakefair 10K footrace. The festival culminates in fireworks bursting above the Capitol dome and reflecting on the waters of Capitol Lake.

Blueberry Banana Smoothie

1 small ripe banana, sliced and frozen
1/4 cup blueberries, frozen
1/4 cup plain yogurt
1/2 cup (or more) fresh orange juice

Combine the banana, blueberries, yogurt and orange juice in a blender and process until smooth. Add additional orange juice if needed for the desired consistency.

SERVES 1

Smoothie Substitutes

Freezing the fruit will make a smoothie cold without diluting it with ice cubes. Any frozen fruit, such as other berries, peaches, or mangoes, may be substituted for or combined with the blueberries. You can increase the nutritional value by using Greek-style yogurt, which typically has more protein than plain yogurt, but you can also use low-fat or nonfat yogurt as well. This is a good way to use bananas that are becoming too ripe; just peel them, cut them into halves, and freeze them in plastic bags to use for smoothies.

Hazelnut French Toast

1 (8-ounce) loaf French bread, sliced 1/2 inch thick
4 eggs
1 cup milk (do not use skim)
1 cup half-and-half
1/2 tablespoon granulated sugar
1 teaspoon vanilla extract
1/4 teaspoon cinnamon
1/4 teaspoon nutmeg
1/8 teaspoon cardamom
6 tablespoons butter, softened
1/2 cup packed light brown sugar
1 tablespoon corn syrup
1/2 cup chopped hazelnuts, toasted

Preheat the oven to 325 degrees. Arrange the bread in a single layer on a baking sheet. Bake for 25 minutes or until dry and golden brown. Arrange the bread tightly in two layers in a buttered 7×11-inch baking dish.

Combine the eggs, milk, half-and-half, granulated sugar, vanilla, cinnamon, nutmeg and cardamom in a bowl and whisk until smooth. Pour over the bread. Chill, covered, for 8 to 24 hours.

Preheat the oven to 350 degrees. Combine the butter, brown sugar and corn syrup in a bowl and mix until smooth. Stir in the hazelnuts. Spoon over the layers in the baking dish. Bake for 1 hour.

SERVES 4

4 eggs, beaten
1/4 cup half-and-half
1/4 cup sugar
6 unbaked (8-inch) Kuchen
   Shells (below)

3 (16-ounce) cans tart cherries
   or sliced peaches, drained
2 cups all-purpose flour
1 cup sugar
1/2 cup (1 stick) unsalted butter
Cinnamon to taste

Preheat the oven to 350 degrees. Beat the eggs, half-and-half and 1/4 cup sugar in a bowl until smooth. Spoon 1/4 cup into each Kuchen Shell and spread to cover evenly. Top each with 1/2 can of the cherries. Mix the flour, 1 cup sugar and the butter in a food processor until crumbly. Sprinkle over the fruit. Bake for 20 minutes or until the edges are light brown. Sprinkle with cinnamon. Cut into wedges and serve warm.

SERVES 12

3 1/2 cups all-purpose flour
1 envelope quick-rising
   dry yeast
1/4 cup sugar

1 teaspoon salt
1 1/4 cups milk
1/4 cup shortening
1 egg, beaten

Combine the flour, yeast, sugar and salt in a food processor fitted with a dough hook. Warm the milk in a saucepan over medium heat. Add the shortening and heat just until the shortening melts. Add to the flour mixture, processing constantly. Mix in the egg. Knead for 1 minute. Shape into a ball and place in a greased bowl, turning to coat evenly. Cover with plastic wrap and let rise in a warm draft-free place for 1 hour or until doubled in bulk.

Divide the dough into six equal portions and roll each into an 8-inch circle on a floured surface. Press into six greased 8-inch foil cake pans. Prick with a fork and cover with towels. Let rise in a warm place for 30 to 45 minutes or until puffy. Use a large spoon to press the bottoms along the edges to better hold the filling.

MAKES 6 (8-INCH) SHELLS

Flax Buttermilk Pancakes

1 egg
2 cups buttermilk
$1/2$ cup flax seed meal
$1/4$ cup sugar

$1/2$ teaspoon baking soda
$1/4$ teaspoon salt
1 cup (or more) all-purpose flour
1 tablespoon baking powder

Whisk the egg in a large mixing bowl until frothy. Add the buttermilk and mix well. Whisk in the flax seed meal, sugar, baking soda and salt. Add the flour and whisk until smooth. Add $1/4$ cup additional flour if needed for the desired consistency. Whisk in the baking powder gently; the batter will be bubbly.

Preheat a skillet or griddle over medium heat. Grease lightly with canola oil if necessary. Spoon the batter by $1/4$ cupfuls onto the skillet. Cook until bubbles rise to the surface and begin to burst. Turn the pancakes over and cook for 1 to 2 minutes longer or until golden brown. Serve with butter and warm maple syrup. You can top the batter with sliced bananas or blueberries as soon as they are poured onto the skillet, if desired.

SERVES 4 TO 6

In-a-Rush Tip

These healthful pancakes are full of fiber and can be a great make-ahead breakfast for rushed mornings. Just make a batch of the pancakes and cool on a baking sheet. Place the cooled pancakes in resealable freezer bags and freeze. To reheat, place two frozen pancakes on a microwave-safe plate and microwave on High for one minute.

Apricot Walnut Pancakes

1/4 cup gluten-free flour
1/2 teaspoon baking soda
1/2 teaspoon salt
1/2 cup walnuts
1 cup quick-cooking oats

1 cup buttermilk
2 eggs
1/4 cup raisins
3 apricot halves, finely chopped

Mix the flour, baking soda, salt and walnuts in a bowl. Combine the oats with the buttermilk in a bowl and mix well. Add the dry ingredients and beat until combined. Add the eggs, raisins and apricots; mix well.

Preheat a griddle over medium heat and grease lightly. Spoon the batter onto the griddle and cook until bubbles rise to the surface and begin to burst. Turn the pancakes over and cook until golden brown.

SERVES 2

Apple Waffles

1/2 cup grated peeled apple
1 carrot, peeled and grated
1/3 cup hazelnuts, chopped
1/4 cup moist currants
1 1/2 cups all-purpose flour
1 tablespoon baking powder
1/3 cup sugar

3/4 teaspoon cinnamon
1/4 teaspoon ginger
1/8 teaspoon salt
1 1/2 cups milk
2 eggs
1 teaspoon vanilla extract
1/4 cup (1/2 stick) butter, melted

Preheat a waffle iron. Mix the apple, carrot, hazelnuts and currants in a bowl. Mix the flour, baking powder, sugar, cinnamon, ginger and salt together.

Beat the eggs with the milk and vanilla in a bowl. Pour over the flour mixture and whisk to combine well. Stir in the apple mixture and butter. Spoon onto the waffle iron and cook using the manufacturer's directions until golden brown.

SERVES 4

Rhubarb Coffee Cake

2 cups all-purpose flour
1 teaspoon baking soda
1/2 teaspoon salt
1/2 cup shortening or
    softened butter
11/2 cups packed brown sugar
1 egg
1 cup sour cream

1 teaspoon vanilla extract
21/2 cups coarsely
    chopped rhubarb
1/2 cup granulated sugar
1/2 cup chopped nuts
1 teaspoon cinnamon
1 tablespoon butter, melted

Preheat the oven to 350 degrees. Mix the flour with the baking soda and salt in a bowl. Cream the shortening and brown sugar in a mixing bowl until light and fluffy. Beat in the egg. Add the dry ingredients alternately with the sour cream, mixing well after each addition. Stir in the vanilla and rhubarb.

Spread the batter in a greased and floured 9×13-inch baking pan. Mix the granulated sugar, nuts, cinnamon and butter in a bowl. Sprinkle over the batter. Bake for 40 to 50 minutes or until the coffee cake tests done.

SERVES 12

Inspired

Laughter, smiles, and joy abound in a magical evening of fun and festivities for foster-care children and families at the **Foster Care Holiday Party**. Junior League of Olympia members are inspired by the experience as they serve the guests dinner, share holiday crafts, and organize games. The evening provides everyone a night of celebration and peace.

Apple and Squash Brunch Cake

3 eggs
1/2 cup (1 stick) butter, softened
1 1/3 cups sugar
1/2 teaspoon vanilla extract
1/2 teaspoon cinnamon
1/4 teaspoon nutmeg
1/4 teaspoon cardamom
1/8 teaspoon ground allspice
2 1/4 cups all-purpose flour
2 teaspoons baking powder

1/2 teaspoon baking soda
1 cup chopped peeled Granny Smith apple
1 cup golden raisins
1 cup walnuts or hazelnuts, chopped
1 cup chopped butternut squash or acorn squash
1/2 cup buttermilk

Preheat the oven to 375 degrees. Combine the eggs, butter, sugar, vanilla, cinnamon, nutmeg, cardamom and allspice in a bowl and whisk until fluffy. Mix the flour, baking powder and baking soda in a bowl. Toss the apple, raisins and walnuts in a bowl.

Place the squash in a microwave-safe dish and microwave on High for 12 minutes or until tender; discard the seeds. Mash the squash with a fork; the mashed squash should measure 3/4 cup. Add the egg mixture and dry ingredients and mix until smooth. Stir in the apple mixture.

Spoon into a greased and floured springform pan or bundt pan. Bake for 2 hours or until the cake tests done. Drizzle with confectioners' sugar glaze, if desired, and serve immediately. This cake freezes well.

SERVES 10

49

Orange Rolls

1 envelope dry yeast
1/2 cup warm water
   (100 to 110 degrees)
1/4 cup sugar
1/2 cup reduced-fat sour cream
2 teaspoons butter, softened
1 egg, lightly beaten
1 teaspoon salt

3 1/2 cups all-purpose flour
2 tablespoons butter, melted
1 cup nuts, chopped (optional)
3/4 cup sugar
2 tablespoons grated
   orange zest
Orange Glaze (page 55)

Dissolve the yeast in the warm water in a large mixing bowl and let stand for 5 minutes. Add 1/4 cup sugar, the sour cream, 2 teaspoons butter, the egg and salt; mix at medium speed until smooth. Add 2 cups of the flour and beat until smooth. Add 1 cup of the remaining flour and stir to form a soft dough. Knead by hand or with a dough hook, finishing by hand, on a floured surface for 10 minutes or until smooth and elastic, adding enough of the remaining 1/2 cup flour one tablespoon at a time as needed to keep the dough from sticking to your hands.

Place the dough in a large bowl coated with nonstick cooking spray and turn to coat the surface. Cover and let rise in a warm draft-free place for 1 1/4 hours or until doubled in bulk and an indentation remains when pressed with two fingers.

Punch down the dough and cover; let stand for 5 minutes. Divide into two equal portions and leave one portion covered as you work with the other. Roll each portion into a 12-inch circle on a floured surface. Brush each with 1 tablespoon of the melted butter.

Sprinkle the nuts and a mixture of 3/4 cup sugar and the orange zest over each circle. Cut each circle into twelve wedges and roll each wedge tightly beginning with the wide end. Place point sides down in a 9×13-inch baking pan coated with nonstick cooking spray. Let rise, covered, for 25 minutes or until doubled in bulk.

Preheat the oven to 350 degrees. Bake the rolls for 25 minutes or until golden brown. Remove the rolls to baking parchment and drizzle with Orange Glaze. Let stand for 20 minutes before serving.

SERVES 24

Squash Rolls

1 cup milk
1/2 cup (1 stick) butter
1 envelope dry yeast
1/4 cup warm water
   (100 to 110 degrees)
2 teaspoons sugar
1 egg

1 (12-ounce) package frozen
   squash, cooked and drained,
   or 1 cup cooked fresh squash
1/2 teaspoon salt
1/2 cup sugar
4 to 6 cups all-purpose flour

Bring the milk to a simmer in a saucepan and then stir in the butter; let cool. Dissolve the yeast in the warm water in a large mixing bowl. Stir in 2 teaspoons sugar gently and let stand for 15 minutes.

Combine the egg, squash, salt and 1/2 cup sugar in a mixing bowl. Add to the yeast mixture. Add enough flour 1 cup at a time to form a very slightly sticky dough, mixing well after each addition; the amount of flour needed will vary depending on the moisture content of the squash and the method of mixing.

Knead the dough by hand on a lightly floured surface for 10 minutes or by machine until satiny smooth. Shape into a ball and place in a bowl sprayed with nonstick cooking spray, turning to coat the surface. Cover with plastic wrap and a towel and let rise in a draft-free place for 2 hours or until doubled in bulk.

Roll the dough into a circle 1/2 inch thick on a floured surface. Cut into small rounds with a glass or biscuit cutter. Place on a parchment paper-lined baking sheet with edges touching. Let rise, covered with plastic wrap, for 1 hour.

Preheat the oven to 375 degrees. Bake the rolls on the center oven rack for 15 minutes or until light brown and hollow-sounding when thumped. Bake, covered with foil, for 5 minutes longer if necessary. Cool slightly in the pan and then remove to a serving platter.

SERVES 12

51

Cherry Scones

1/3 cup dried cherries
1/2 cup boiling water
1 1/2 cups all-purpose flour
1/2 tablespoon baking powder
1/4 teaspoon cream of tartar
1/4 teaspoon salt
2 tablespoons sugar
1/4 cup (1/2 stick)
   butter, softened

1 egg yolk
1/4 cup sour cream
1/3 cup plus 1 tablespoon
   half-and-half
1 teaspoon almond extract
1 egg white, lightly beaten
2 teaspoons sugar

Preheat the oven the 400 degrees. Combine the dried cherries and water in a heatproof bowl and soak for 10 minutes. Mix the flour, baking powder, cream of tartar, salt and 2 tablespoons sugar in a large bowl. Cut in the butter with a pastry blender until the mixture resembles coarse crumbs.

Combine the egg yolk, sour cream, half-and-half and almond extract in a bowl and mix well. Add to the crumb mixture and stir to form a soft dough. Mix in the cherries and knead lightly on a floured surface just until the dough can be easily handled.

Shape into a ball and then pat into a 6-inch circle on a greased baking sheet; cut into six wedges. Brush with the egg white and sprinkle with 2 teaspoons sugar. Bake for 15 to 20 minutes or until golden brown.

SERVES 6

Buttermilk Biscuits

2 cups unbleached
   all-purpose flour
1 tablespoon baking powder
$1/2$ teaspoon baking soda
1 tablespoon sugar
$1/2$ teaspoon salt
5 tablespoons unsalted butter,
   chilled and chopped

$1^1/2$ cups buttermilk, chilled
1 cup unbleached
   all-purpose flour
2 tablespoons unsalted
   butter, melted

Preheat the oven to 500 degrees. Combine 2 cups flour with the baking powder, baking soda, sugar and salt in a bowl or food processor; mix by hand or pulse for six 1-second intervals. Add 5 tablespoons butter and mix with a pastry blender, fork or food processor; the mixture should resemble coarse cornmeal. Add the buttermilk and mix with a spatula. Do not overmix; the dough should be loose, almost like cottage cheese.

Place 1 cup flour in a large bowl or on a baking sheet. Scoop the dough by $1/4$ cupfuls and drop into the flour. Toss the dough balls gently from hand to hand to form a light, fluffy floured ball; do not knead the dough. Place the dough balls in a greased baking pan, filling the pan and leaving no space between the dough balls.

Brush the tops gently with 2 tablespoons butter. Bake for 15 minutes or until golden brown. Cool in the pan for several minutes and then invert onto a serving plate.

SERVES 12

Presto Gouda Beer Bread

3 cups self-rising flour
3 tablespoons sugar
1 (12-ounce) can beer, at room temperature
1 cup (4 ounces) shredded Gouda cheese or other cheese

Preheat the oven to 350 degrees. Combine the flour, sugar and beer in a bowl and mix well. Place half the dough in a greased and floured 5×9-inch loaf pan. Sprinkle with 3/4 cup of the Gouda cheese. Add the remaining dough and top with the remaining 1/4 cup cheese. Bake for 1 hour. Remove to a wire rack to cool before slicing to serve.

MAKES 1 LOAF

Cheese Change-Up

This versatile recipe can be changed to fit your menu. To serve it with a pot of chili, use Pepper Jack cheese and Mexican beer. For a stronger cheese flavor, use sharp Cheddar cheese in place of the Gouda. Substitute crumbled herbed feta cheese for a Mediterranean twist. You must not, however, substitute other flours for the self-rising flour, as it is essential.

Cranberry Orange Bread

2 cups all-purpose flour
1 cup sugar
1 1/2 teaspoons baking powder
1 1/2 teaspoons baking soda
1 teaspoon salt
1 large orange, cut into quarters

2 tablespoons shortening
1 egg, beaten
1 cup pecans or
    walnuts, chopped
1 cup fresh cranberries,
    cut into halves

Sift the flour, sugar, baking powder, baking soda and salt together. Place the unpeeled orange in a food processor and pulse until puréed. Place the shortening in a measuring cup and add enough water to measure 3/4 cup. Add to the orange. Add the egg and process until well mixed.

Add the dry ingredients to the orange mixture and pulse until well mixed. Add the pecans and cranberries and pulse two or three times. Pour into a greased loaf pan and let stand for 30 minutes.

Preheat the oven to 350 degrees. Bake for 1 hour. Remove to a wire rack to cool.

MAKES 1 LOAF

Orange Glaze

3/4 cup sugar
1/4 cup (1/2 stick) butter

2 tablespoons fresh orange juice
1/2 cup reduced-fat sour cream

Mix the sugar, butter and orange juice in a small saucepan. Bring to a boil over medium-high heat. Boil for 3 minutes or until the sugar dissolves completely, stirring occasionally. Cool slightly and then stir in the sour cream. Use to glaze Orange Rolls (page 50) or other breads.

MAKES 1 1/2 CUPS

Soups

SOUPS

◀ SZECHUAN CARROT SOUP AND FRESH VEGETABLE
ROLLS WITH SWEET CHILI SAUCE

Curry Chicken Soup

6 boneless skinless chicken
    thighs, or 3 boneless
    skinless chicken breasts,
    cut into 1-inch pieces
2 tablespoons olive oil
1 large sweet onion,
    coarsely chopped
1 red bell pepper,
    coarsely chopped

3 ribs celery, coarsely chopped
Salt and pepper to taste
8 cups chicken broth
3 carrots, cut into $1/2$-inch pieces
$1/2$ cup uncooked wild rice
$1/2$ cup golden raisins
1 to 3 tablespoons curry
    powder, or to taste
1 turnip, cut into $1/2$-inch pieces

Brown the chicken in the olive oil in a large saucepan. Add the onion and bell pepper and sauté until the onion is translucent. Add the celery, salt and pepper. Stir in the broth, carrots, wild rice, raisins and curry powder.

Cook for 1 hour or just until the wild rice is tender. Add the turnip and cook for 15 minutes longer. Ladle into soup bowls and garnish with fresh cilantro.

SERVES 8

Inspiration

Imagine having to choose between buying food and clothes or school supplies. Each year many guardians are faced with this choice. Teachers report that children begin school without the needed supplies or clothing. Seeing this need, the Junior League of Olympia (JLO) was instrumental in the formation of **The Little Red Schoolhouse** in 1991. JLO and community partners teamed up with the inspiration for every child to start school with the basic school supplies, clean clothes, and a backpack.

Creamy Chicken and Wild Rice Soup

1 cup uncooked wild rice
Salt to taste
4 cups water
1/4 cup (1/2 stick) butter
1/2 cup finely chopped onion
1 cup chopped carrots
6 tablespoons all-purpose flour

1 teaspoon Italian seasoning
1/2 teaspoon salt
1/4 teaspoon pepper
3 cups (or more) chicken broth
2 cups chopped cooked chicken
1/2 cup frozen peas
1 cup half-and-half or 2% milk

Combine the rice and salt to taste with the water in a saucepan and bring to a boil. Cover and reduce the heat. Simmer for 50 to 60 minutes or until the rice is tender and the water is absorbed.

Melt the butter in a 2-quart saucepan over medium heat. Add the onion and carrots and sauté for 5 minutes or until tender. Reduce the heat to low and stir in the flour, Italian seasoning, 1/2 teaspoon salt and the pepper. Cook until bubby. Stir in the chicken broth.

Cook until the mixture comes to a boil and thickens, stirring occasionally. Add the wild rice, chicken, peas and half-and-half. Cook until heated through, adding additional chicken broth if needed for the desired consistency. Adjust the seasonings and ladle into soup bowls.

SERVES 6

59

Hood Canal Shrimp Stew

2 cups chopped onions
2 cups chopped celery
1 cup chopped green
   bell pepper
2 garlic cloves, chopped
Pinch of red pepper flakes
1/4 cup (or more) canola oil
1 (6-ounce) can tomato paste

1 pound shrimp, chopped
Salt and black pepper to taste
1 1/2 cups shrimp stock or
   clam juice
1/4 cup chopped green
   onion tops
1/4 cup chopped parsley
Cooked white rice

Sauté the onions, celery, bell pepper, garlic and red pepper flakes in the canola oil in a saucepan until the vegetables are translucent. Stir in the tomato paste. Add the shrimp, salt and black pepper. Sauté until the shrimp are pink, stirring or shaking the saucepan several times.

Add the stock and simmer for 15 minutes. Add the green onions and parsley and cook for 5 minutes longer. Serve over cooked white rice in soup bowls. You can substitute wine for half the shrimp stock or clam juice, if preferred.

SERVES 4 TO 8

Clam Chowder

8 slices thick-cut bacon,
   chopped
1/2 cup (1 stick) butter
1/2 large onion, chopped
1 cup chopped celery
1/4 cup all-purpose flour
4 (6-ounce) cans chopped clams

1 (16-ounce) bottle clam juice
4 large russet potatoes, peeled
   and chopped
3 cups milk
1/2 cup half-and-half
Salt and pepper to taste

Cook the bacon in a large heavy saucepan over medium-high heat until crisp; drain the drippings from the saucepan. Add the butter, onion and celery and sauté until the onion is tender. Stir in the flour and cook for 3 minutes, stirring constantly.

Drain the clams, reserving the liquid in a 2-cup measuring cup. Add enough of the bottled clam juice to measure 2 cups. Add to the saucepan and mix well. Add the potatoes and bring to a boil. Reduce the heat and simmer for 20 minutes or until the potatoes are tender.

Add the clams, milk and half-and-half. Cook until heated through; do not boil. Season with salt and pepper. Ladle into soup bowls.

SERVES 6

61

Salmon Chowder with Cilantro

4 ounces thick-cut bacon, cut into 1/8-inch pieces

2 sweet onions, cut into quarters and thinly sliced

1 1/2 teaspoons coriander

1 pound sweet potatoes, peeled and cut into 1/4-inch pieces

1 (24-ounce) bottle clam juice

1 1/2 pounds skinless salmon fillets, cut into 1/2-inch pieces

2 cups half-and-half

1/2 cup lightly packed fresh cilantro, chopped

2 teaspoons salt, or to taste

1/2 teaspoon freshly ground black pepper, or to taste

Dash of cayenne pepper, or to taste

Sauté the bacon until light brown in a large stockpot over medium heat, stirring frequently. Remove with a slotted spoon, reserving the drippings in the stockpot. Add the onions to the drippings and sauté for 5 minutes or until tender.

Stir in the coriander, sweet potatoes and clam juice. Bring to a boil over high heat. Reduce the heat to medium and cook for 5 minutes or just until the sweet potatoes are tender.

Reduce the heat to low and add the salmon. Cook for 5 minutes or just until the salmon is firm and opaque. Stir in the half-and-half and cook until heated through. Add the bacon and cilantro and season with the salt, black pepper and cayenne pepper. Ladle into soup bowls.

SERVES 8 TO 10

Northwest Southwest Seafood Stew

1 tablespoon vegetable oil
1 large onion, chopped
1 red bell pepper, chopped
2 fresh Anaheim chiles, seeded
   and chopped
12 mussels, scrubbed
12 clams, scrubbed
2 green onions,
   coarsely chopped

3 (14-ounce) cans unsweetened
   light coconut milk
12 large shrimp, peeled
   and deveined
1/2 cup minced cilantro
Juice of 1 lime
Salt and pepper to taste

Heat the vegetable oil in a large saucepan over medium heat. Add the onion, bell pepper and chiles and sauté for 5 minutes or until tender. Add the mussels, clams, green onions and coconut milk. Bring to a boil and then reduce to a simmer.

Add the shrimp, cilantro and lime juice. Simmer, covered, for 10 minutes or just until the clams and mussels open. Season with salt and pepper and discard any clams or mussels that did not open. Ladle into soup bowls.

SERVES 4

Can You Dig 'Em?

A true clam aficionado may well enjoy the chase as well as the taste of this elusive mollusk. Clamming season is open for only a few days at a time. At those times, clam diggers flock to the misty beaches where the Pacific razor clam is abundant on the edge of the surf line, as well as in the sheltered areas along the coast. Digging for razor clams is a tradition for many Northwest families. Children are thrilled to locate the clams squirting sand and water out of a hole. Diggers move quickly in the surf, as the clams burrow extremely quickly into the soft sand. Clam digging can be wet and messy, but well worth the adventure.

Reprinted with permission of *The Olympian/* Tony Overman

Minestrone

1 pound bulk Italian sausage
3 tablespoons olive oil
1 cup sliced celery
1 cup chopped onion
3/4 cup sliced carrots
1 teaspoon salt
3 garlic cloves
3 cups tomato purée
7 cups chicken stock
1/2 cup chopped fresh parsley
2 teaspoons oregano
11/2 teaspoons Worcestershire
   sauce

1/2 teaspoon red pepper flakes
3/4 cup uncooked shell pasta
   (optional)
1 (15-ounce) can cannellini
   beans, drained and rinsed
1 cup sliced zucchini
4 cups finely chopped
   fresh spinach
1/2 cup fresh basil, sliced
Freshly ground black pepper
   to taste
3/4 cup (3 ounces) grated
   Parmesan cheese

Brown the Italian sausage in a skillet; drain on paper towels. Heat the olive oil in a large stockpot over medium-high heat. Add the celery, onion and carrots. Reduce the heat to low and cook, covered, for 10 minutes. Mash the salt and garlic to a paste and add to the stockpot along with the tomato purée, stock, parsley, oregano, Worcestershire sauce and red pepper flakes.

Bring the soup to a boil and then reduce the heat to a simmer. Simmer for 45 minutes. Add the pasta and sausage and cook for 15 minutes. Add the beans, zucchini, spinach, basil and black pepper. Cook for 15 minutes longer. Ladle into heated soup bowls and sprinkle with the cheese.

SERVES 10

Chef Kyle Fulwiler

As the chef at the Washington State Executive Mansion, Kyle Fulwiler was often called upon to create delicious meals for important guests and noteworthy events. Chef Fulwiler took advantage of the fresh produce the area has to offer to make this flavorful and robust minestrone.

8 ounces thinly sliced bacon,
cut into 1-inch pieces
12 ounces hot Italian sausage,
casings removed and sausage
cut into 1/4-inch pieces
1 pound lean ground beef
1 large onion, chopped
1 bell pepper, chopped
2 garlic cloves, minced
1 cup dark red wine
1/2 cup Worcestershire sauce

11/2 teaspoons chili powder
1 teaspoon dry mustard
1 teaspoon celery seeds
1/2 teaspoon salt
11/2 teaspoons freshly
ground pepper
2 (28-ounce) cans diced tomatoes
1 (15-ounce) can pinto beans
1 (15-ounce) can kidney beans
1 (15-ounce) can
garbanzo beans

Brown the bacon in a large stockpot. Remove to paper towels using a slotted spoon and pour off the drippings. Repeat this process twice more with the Italian sausage and the ground beef, leaving a film of oil in the stockpot.

Add the onion, bell pepper and garlic to the stockpot and sauté over medium heat for 3 minutes. Add the wine and Worcestershire sauce. Simmer, uncovered, for 10 minutes. Stir in the chili powder, dry mustard, celery seeds, salt and pepper. Simmer for 10 minutes.

Add the undrained tomatoes, bacon, Italian sausage and beef to the stockpot. Bring to a boil and then reduce the heat to a simmer. Simmer for 30 minutes, stirring occasionally. Add the undrained pinto beans, kidney beans and garbanzo beans. Bring to a boil and then reduce the heat to medium-low. Simmer for 1 hour, stirring occasionally.

Ladle into soup bowls and garnish with shredded Cheddar cheese.

SERVES 6 TO 8

Black Bean Chili

2 chicken breasts, cooked (optional)
3 (15-ounce) cans black beans
1 onion, chopped
1 red bell pepper, chopped
1 garlic clove, minced

Olive oil
1 (16-ounce) can crushed tomatoes
1 teaspoon ground cumin
1 teaspoon chili powder
1/2 teaspoon salt

Shred the chicken and drain the black beans. Sauté the onion, bell pepper and garlic in a small amount of olive oil in a large saucepan until tender. Add the remaining ingredients; mix well. Simmer for 30 minutes. You may also cook in a slow cooker on Low for 8 hours. Ladle into serving bowls and garnish with shredded cheese and sour cream.

SERVES 8

Vegetarian Chili

1 (12-ounce) can vegetable juice cocktail
1 cup uncooked bulgur
1 large sweet onion, chopped
4 garlic cloves, crushed
2 tablespoons olive oil
1 cup chopped carrots
1 cup chopped celery
2 teaspoons chili powder
1 teaspoon cumin
1 teaspoon basil

Salt and black pepper to taste
Dash of cayenne pepper
1 cup chopped bell pepper
3 (15-ounce) cans kidney beans, pinto beans and/or black beans
2 cups chopped fresh tomatoes
Juice of 1/2 lemon
3 tablespoons tomato paste
3 tablespoons dry red wine

Bring the vegetable juice cocktail to a boil in a saucepan. Pour over the bulgur in a heatproof bowl and let stand, covered, for 15 minutes.

Sauté the onion and garlic in the olive oil in a large saucepan until the onion is translucent. Stir in the next eight ingredients. Sauté until the carrots are tender. Add the bell pepper and sauté until tender. Add the remaining ingredients. Cook over low heat until heated through. Ladle into soup bowls and garnish with cheese and parsley.

SERVES 6 TO 8

Waterstreet Artichoke Truffle Soup

3 long-stemmed Italian
   artichokes
1/4 cup olive oil
1 cup chopped onion
1/2 cup chopped celery
1/2 cup white wine

4 cups chicken stock or
   vegetable stock (do not
   substitute broth)
4 cups heavy cream
Salt and pepper to taste
White truffle oil for drizzling

Cut off the artichoke stems. Peel off the stringy outer layers of the stems with a paring knife or vegetable peeler to reveal the tender white portion. Slice the white portion thinly and place in a measuring cup. Snap off and discard the four outer layers of the artichokes. Cut each artichoke into halves and place cut side down on a work surface. Cut off and discard the top two-thirds of each leaf. Scrape out and discard the choke (fine fuzzy portion in the center). Slice the remainder of the artichokes into thin slices and then chop the slices. Place in the measuring cup and measure 3 cups of artichoke.

Heat the olive oil in a large stockpot over medium heat. Add the artichokes, onion and celery. Sauté until the vegetables are tender. Add the wine and cook until slightly reduced. Add the stock and cream. Simmer, uncovered, for 20 minutes. Season with salt and pepper. Ladle into soup bowls and drizzle with white truffle oil.

You can also process the soup in a food processor or blender or with an immersion blender for a smoother soup.

SERVES 8

Chef Jeff Taylor

Jeff Taylor, the owner of Waterstreet Café and Bar in Olympia, serves this warm and savory soup to eager customers on cold and rainy days. The long stems of the artichokes have a rich and meaty flavor and add a texture and taste that makes it so heavenly.

Autumn Ham and Bean Soup

1 ham bone or precooked
   ham shank
1 (1-pound) package dried
   bean mix, sorted and rinsed
Chicken stock
1 cup chopped cooked ham
2 large carrots, chopped
2 large ribs celery, chopped
1 green or red bell
   pepper, chopped

1 yellow onion, chopped
2 garlic cloves, minced
1 (14-ounce) can
   diced tomatoes
4 teaspoons chopped fresh basil
4 teaspoons fresh thyme
2 teaspoons dried oregano
2 teaspoons salt, or to taste
1/2 teaspoon cracked pepper

Combine the ham bone with enough water to cover in a large stockpot or slow cooker. Simmer over very low heat for several hours or cook on Low for 6 to 8 hours. Chill in the refrigerator and skim the surface if time permits.

Combine the beans with enough cold water to cover in a bowl and soak for 1 1/2 to 2 hours; drain.

Strain the ham broth and combine with enough chicken stock to measure 8 cups. Pour in a stockpot. Add the beans, ham, carrots, celery, bell pepper, onion, garlic, tomatoes, basil, thyme, oregano, salt and pepper. Bring to a boil and then reduce the heat. Simmer for 1 hour, adding water if necessary for the desired consistency. Adjust the seasonings and ladle into soup bowls.

You can also purée the soup in batches in a blender and combine with 1 cup heavy cream in the stockpot. Heat just to serving temperature; do not boil.

SERVES 10 TO 12

Szechuan Carrot Soup

1 large onion, coarsely chopped
3 garlic cloves, coarsely chopped
1/2 teaspoon red pepper flakes, or to taste
1 tablespoon vegetable oil
2 tablespoons grated fresh ginger

1 pound carrots, chopped
2 tablespoons peanut butter or cashew butter
1 tablespoon soy sauce
1 tablespoon sesame oil
Juice of 1 lime
Salt and pepper to taste
2 to 3 cups milk

Sauté the onion, garlic and red pepper flakes in the vegetable oil in a saucepan until the onion is tender. Add the ginger, carrots and enough water to cover the vegetables. Cook over medium heat until the carrots are tender. Purée in a food processor.

Combine the puréed mixture with the peanut butter, soy sauce, sesame oil, lime juice, salt and pepper in the saucepan. Add enough of the milk to reach the desired consistency. Cook until heated through. Ladle into soup bowls and serve immediately or chill in the refrigerator and serve cold.

SERVES 4 TO 6

Washington State Executive Mansion

There may not be any other view to rival the scenery from the Washington State Executive Mansion. Perched on a slight hilltop on the Washington State Capitol campus, the mansion overlooks Capitol Lake, which reflects the legislative dome, the serene water of Puget Sound, and the stunning Olympic Mountains. Washington State governors have made the red brick Georgian-style mansion their home since 1910, even though it was originally built as a temporary state house to greet important visitors during the 1909 Alaska/Yukon/Pacific Exposition.

Corn and Cheddar Chowder

2 cups salted water
1 large potato, peeled and chopped
1 bay leaf
1/2 teaspoon cumin seeds
1/4 teaspoon dried sage
3 tablespoons butter
1 small onion, finely chopped
3 tablespoons all-purpose flour
1 1/2 cups heavy cream

Kernels from 2 ears of fresh corn, or 1 (10-ounce) package frozen corn
3 tablespoons chopped parsley
2 tablespoons chopped chives
1/4 teaspoon nutmeg
Salt and pepper to taste
1 1/2 cups (6 ounces) shredded sharp Cheddar cheese
5 tablespoons dry white wine
Milk

Bring the salted water to a boil in a large saucepan. Add the potato, bay leaf, cumin and sage. Cook for 15 minutes or just until the potato is tender.

Melt the butter in a saucepan over medium heat. Add the onion and sauté until translucent. Stir in the flour. Add the cream and cook until thickened and smooth, whisking constantly. Add to the potato mixture along with the corn.

Stir in the parsley, chives, nutmeg, salt and pepper. Reduce the heat and simmer for 10 minutes. Stir in the Cheddar cheese and cook until melted.

Add the wine. Add milk if needed for the desired consistency. Adjust the seasonings and discard the bay leaf. Ladle into soup bowls and garnish with additional chives and parsley.

SERVES 4 TO 6

Onion Soup au Gratin

1/4 cup (1/2 stick)
   unsalted butter
4 large red onions, cut into
   halves and thinly sliced
2 tablespoons sugar
4 cups chicken stock
2 cups beef stock

Salt and pepper to taste
2 tablespoons ruby port
Splash of balsamic vinegar
6 slices dry crusty bread
Shredded Gruyère cheese or
   Swiss cheese

Melt the butter in a stockpot. Add the onions and cook, covered, over low heat for 20 minutes. Sprinkle the sugar over the onions and toss to coat evenly. Cook, uncovered, for 25 minutes or until the onions are golden brown.

Mix the chicken stock and beef stock in a bowl. Add 3 cups of the stock mixture to the stockpot and season with salt and pepper. Simmer, uncovered, for 15 minutes. Add the remaining 3 cups stock and the wine. Simmer for about 40 minutes. Adjust the seasonings and add the balsamic vinegar.

Preheat the broiler. Ladle the soup into six ovenproof bowls. Top each serving with a slice of the bread and cheese. Broil until the cheese melts. Serve immediately.

SERVES 6

71

Potato and Cheese Soup

6 red potatoes, peeled
1 tablespoon butter
1 cup chopped onion
1 garlic clove, finely chopped
2 tablespoons all-purpose flour
3 cups chicken broth
1 cup water

1 cup (4 ounces) shredded
    Cheddar cheese
8 ounces American
    cheese, cubed
1/2 cup beer (optional)
2 tablespoons sherry (optional)
Salt and white pepper to taste

Combine the potatoes with enough water to cover in a large stockpot. Bring to a boil and then reduce the heat to medium-low. Simmer for 10 minutes or until the potatoes are tender. Drain, cool and chop the potatoes.

Melt the butter in a large saucepan. Add the onion and garlic and sauté until the onion is translucent. Add the flour and cook until smooth, stirring constantly.

Add the broth and 1 cup water gradually. Bring to a low boil, stirring constantly. Add the potatoes. Stir in the Cheddar cheese and American cheese gradually. Add the beer and wine and reduce the heat. Heat the soup to serving temperature. Season with salt and white pepper and ladle into soup bowls. Garnish with bacon crumbles and steamed broccoli florets.

SERVES 4

Palates of Northwest Beer Drinkers

Great beer is one of the regional trademarks of the Pacific Northwest, where craft brewing was born. The microbrewery culture is dedicated to the development of unique and complex flavors rather than mass production and wide distribution. The Olympia Brewing Company began brewing the very popular Pacific Northwest brand Olympia Beer in 1896 and eventually expanded the market nationwide. The excellence of its beer has been attributed to the exceptional quality of the water—hence the slogan "It's the Water." Olympia continues its brewing legacy with many award-winning and uniquely crafted local microbrews.

Tomato Mushroom Soup

1 (28-ounce) can diced
   fire-roasted tomatoes
1 onion, cut into
   quarters
3 garlic cloves
8 to 16 ounces portobello
   mushrooms or crimini
   mushrooms
3 tablespoons basil

3 tablespoons fresh herbes
   de Provence
4 cups (1 quart) vegetable
   broth, chicken broth,
   mushroom broth or beef broth
1 (6-ounce) can tomato paste
1/2 teaspoon salt
1/2 teaspoon pepper
2 cups half-and-half

Purée the tomatoes in a food processor. Add the onion, garlic, mushrooms, basil and herbes de Provence and process until smooth. Combine with the broth, tomato paste, salt and pepper in a large saucepan and mix well.

Bring to a boil over medium heat, stirring frequently. Reduce the heat and simmer for 20 to 30 minutes, adding the half-and-half during the last 5 minutes of cooking time and continuing to simmer until heated through.

Ladle into soup bowls and garnish with shredded cheese and sour cream. You can reserve some of the diced tomatoes to add later for a chunkier soup. You may also substitute soy milk or other milk for the half-and-half. This soup can be made in a slow cooker and cooked on Low for 6 to 8 hours.

SERVES 6 TO 8

73

French
Tomato Soup

2 large onions, chopped
2 slices bacon, chopped
1 tablespoon butter
4 cups chicken broth
1 cup chopped canned tomatoes
1 tablespoon tomato purée
Juice of $1/2$ lemon
2 or 3 strips of lemon zest
1 teaspoon sugar
1 teaspoon parsley
1 teaspoon basil
$1/4$ teaspoon thyme

Sauté the onions and bacon in a stockpot until brown. Add the butter. Mix the broth, tomatoes, tomato purée, lemon juice, lemon zest, sugar, parsley, basil and thyme in a bowl. Add to the stockpot and mix well.

Bring the soup to a boil and then reduce the heat. Simmer for 30 minutes. Process in a food processor until puréed. Ladle into soup bowls and garnish with chopped fresh basil. Serve with French bread.

SERVES 4

2 tablespoons canola oil
4 garlic cloves, minced
1/2 cup shiitake mushrooms,
   sliced
1 cup fresh spinach leaves
4 cups vegetable stock

1 to 2 teaspoons low-sodium
   soy sauce
Tofu Won Tons (below)
2 tablespoons chopped
   green onions

Heat the canola oil in a 4^1/2-quart saucepan. Add the garlic and sauté until golden brown. Add the mushrooms and sauté until tender. Add the spinach, stock and soy sauce. Bring to a boil and then reduce the heat. Simmer just until the spinach is tender.

Return the soup to a boil. Add Tofu Won Tons and cook for 5 minutes. Ladle into soup bowls and sprinkle with the green onions. Serve with jasmine rice, if desired.

SERVES 4 TO 6

4 ounces firm tofu, mashed
1 egg, beaten (optional)
2 tablespoons chopped cilantro

1/4 teaspoon salt
Pinch of pepper
12 to 16 won ton wrappers

Combine the tofu, egg, cilantro, salt and pepper in a bowl and mix well. Arrange the won ton wrappers on a work surface and place 1 teaspoon of the tofu mixture in the center of each.

Brush the edges of the won tons with water and fold each in half diagonally to form triangles; press the edges to seal. Brush the two corners of the wide side with water and press together.

Use the won tons in a recipe immediately or store in the freezer for future use. Bring frozen won tons to room temperature and cook just before serving time.

MAKES 12 TO 16

Baked Brie Soup

1 tablespoon butter
1 cup chopped mushrooms
1 shallot or small onion, chopped
1 garlic clove, crushed
4 cups chicken stock
1/2 cup heavy cream

Salt and white pepper to taste
8 ounces Brie cheese, rind removed and cheese cut into 8 pieces
8 (1/4-inch) slices baguette, toasted

Preheat the oven to 400 degrees. Melt the butter in a heavy medium saucepan over medium heat. Add the mushrooms, shallot and garlic. Sauté for 3 minutes. Stir in the stock and bring to a boil. Cook until reduced by one-third. Strain into a saucepan, discarding the vegetables. Add the cream. Bring to a boil and cook until slightly thickened. Season with salt and white pepper.

Place one piece of the Brie cheese in each of four ovenproof bowls. Ladle the soup into the bowls and float two baguette slices in each. Top each with one of the remaining Brie cheese pieces. Bake for 5 minutes or until the cheese is bubbly.

SERVES 4

Summer Gazpacho

1 (42-ounce) can tomatoes
1 (24-ounce) can tomato juice
1/2 cup chopped bell pepper
1/2 cup chopped red onion
1/2 cup chopped celery
1/2 cup chopped cucumber

1/4 cup rosé
1/4 cup olive oil
Juice of 1 lime
1/2 teaspoon ground cumin
1/2 teaspoon chopped chives
1/2 teaspoon basil

Combine the tomatoes, tomato juice, bell pepper, onion, celery and cucumber in a food mill, blender or food processor. Process until smooth. Combine with the wine, olive oil, lime juice, cumin, chives and basil in a bowl and mix well. Chill for several hours.

Ladle the soup into soup bowls. Serve with toppings of choice such as chopped tomatoes, avocados, cucumber, onion, bell pepper, croutons and/or sour cream.

SERVES 10 TO 12

Salads

SALADS

◀ SMOKED SALMON COBB SALAD

Pear and Walnut Salad with Blue Cheese

3 tablespoons sugar
1 tablespoon water
1/2 cup walnut halves
8 cups torn salad greens
2 small firm pears, thinly sliced
1/2 cup crumbled blue cheese
Shallot Dressing (below)

Sprinkle the sugar into an 8-inch skillet over medium-high heat. Cook until the sugar melts and becomes amber in color, shaking frequently. Add the water; the sugar will harden. Cook until the sugar liquefies again, stirring constantly. Add the walnuts and stir to coat evenly. Let cool to room temperature.

Combine the salad greens, pears and three-fourths of the walnuts in a large bowl. Add the Shallot Dressing and toss gently. Sprinkle with the blue cheese and the remaining walnuts.

SERVES 8 TO 10

80

Shallot Dressing

1/2 cup olive oil or vegetable oil
2 tablespoons lemon juice
1 large shallot, minced
1/2 teaspoon sugar
1/2 teaspoon pepper

Combine the olive oil, lemon juice, shallot, sugar and pepper in a container with a tight-fitting lid. Shake to mix well.

MAKES 3/4 CUP

Roasted Artichoke and Potato Salad

2 1/2 pounds small red potatoes, cut into quarters
2 (9-ounce) packages frozen artichoke hearts, thawed and drained
10 garlic cloves, cut into halves lengthwise
1/4 cup olive oil
1 teaspoon kosher salt
1/4 teaspoon freshly ground pepper
1/4 cup fresh lemon juice
1 teaspoon grated lemon zest
2 tablespoons chopped fresh parsley

Preheat the oven to 425 degrees. Combine the potatoes with the artichoke hearts, garlic, olive oil, kosher salt and pepper in a 9×13-inch baking dish; toss to coat well. Roast for 30 to 40 minutes or until the potatoes are tender and brown, stirring after 20 minutes. Remove from the oven and mash some of the garlic cloves with a fork. Let cool for several minutes in the baking dish.

Mix the lemon juice, lemon zest and parsley in a small bowl. Combine with the potato mixture in a serving bowl and toss to coat evenly. Serve warm or at room temperature.

SERVES 8

81

Potluck Perfect

This recipe is perfect for a potluck or buffet. The light dressing of olive oil and lemon juice becomes more flavorful at room temperature, and the salad will not get soggy as it sits. If you have leftovers, reheat them in a skillet over medium-high heat and serve them with scrambled or poached eggs for a new twist on hash browns.

Arugula Salad with Pecorino-Romano Cheese and Toasted Walnuts

1/2 cup walnut halves
1 teaspoon butter
1 bunch arugula
1 package mâche or
    oak leaf lettuce

Sherry Dijon Vinaigrette (below)
1/2 cup (2 ounces) coarsely
    grated pecorino-Romano
    cheese, or to taste

Toast the walnuts in the butter in a small skillet over low heat until golden brown.

Cut off and discard the bottom one-third of the arugula; chop the arugula. Cut off and discard the root ends of the mâche. Spin the greens dry in a salad spinner.

Combine the greens with enough of the Sherry Dijon Vinaigrette to coat well. Spoon onto serving plates and top with the cheese and walnuts.

SERVES 4 TO 6

Sherry Dijon Vinaigrette

1 1/2 tablespoons sherry vinegar
    or tarragon vinegar
1 garlic clove, minced
1/4 teaspoon salt

1 teaspoon Dijon mustard
6 tablespoons walnut oil or
    extra-virgin olive oil

Combine the sherry vinegar, garlic and salt in a bowl and whisk to mix well. Let stand for 15 minutes. Stir in the Dijon mustard and walnut oil. Adjust the vinegar if necessary.

MAKES 1/2 CUP

Green Bean Salad with Feta Cheese and Walnuts

1 1/2 pounds fresh green beans, trimmed and cut into 1-inch pieces
Salt to taste
3/4 cup olive oil
1/4 cup white wine vinegar
1 garlic clove, minced

3/4 teaspoon salt
1/4 teaspoon freshly ground pepper
1 cup crumbled feta cheese
1 cup chopped red onion
1 cup toasted walnuts, chopped
Salad greens (optional)

Combine the beans with enough salted water to cover in a saucepan. Bring to a boil and cook for about 4 minutes or until tender-crisp; drain. Plunge the green beans in ice water to stop the cooking process.

Combine the olive oil, vinegar, garlic, 3/4 teaspoon salt and the pepper in a large bowl and whisk until smooth. Drain the beans and add to the dressing with the cheese, onion and walnuts; toss to coat well. Chill for 1 hour. Serve over salad greens.

SERVES 8

Inspirational

Kids on the Block offers elementary-age children alternative ways to handle important social issues and build diversity awareness. A team of Junior League of Olympia members reaches more than six hundred children in Thurston County annually. The use of puppetry and carefully worded scripts engage the children in a lesson of compassion and understanding for one another.

Roasted Beet Salad

4 beets, cut into quarters
1 tablespoon olive oil
1/2 teaspoon sea salt or kosher salt, or to taste
1/8 teaspoon freshly ground pepper
1/4 cup crumbled goat cheese
1/4 cup toasted pecans, chopped

Preheat the oven to 425 degrees. Boil the beets in enough water to cover in a saucepan until just barely tender; drain. Plunge the beets in ice water to stop the cooking process. Let stand until cool enough to handle and then drain on paper towels. Peel the beets and cut into bite-size pieces. Toss with the olive oil, sea salt and pepper in a bowl.

Place in a baking dish. Bake for 20 minutes. Let cool to room temperature. Combine with the cheese and pecans in a serving bowl and toss to coat evenly.

As a variation, you can toss 1 cup of arugula or mixed greens with a small amount of sherry vinegar, olive oil, salt and pepper and top with the beet salad.

SERVES 4

84

Avocado Caesar Salad

1 ripe avocado
1 large garlic clove, crushed and minced
1/4 cup olive oil
Chopped anchovies to taste
1/4 teaspoon salt, or to taste
1 head romaine, torn
1/3 cup fresh lemon juice
1/4 cup (1 ounce) grated Parmesan cheese

Mash the avocado in a large salad bowl. Add the garlic, olive oil, anchovies and salt and mix well. Add the romaine and toss to coat. Add the lemon juice gradually. Adjust the seasoning and top with the Parmesan cheese.

SERVES 4

Grilled Caesar Salad

2 heads romaine
1 tablespoon olive oil

1/2 cup Caesar Dressing (below)
1/4 cup croutons, crumbled

Preheat the grill to high or to at least 400 degrees. Split the heads of romaine lengthwise. Brush the cut sides lightly with the olive oil. Place the lettuce cut side down on the open grill using tongs. Grill for 2 minutes or until the lettuce is marked by the grill and is slightly wilted on the edges. Remove to a serving platter and drizzle with the Caesar Dressing; top with the croutons.

SERVES 4

Caesar Dressing

3 tablespoons lemon juice
1 tablespoon cider vinegar
1 tablespoon Worcestershire
　　sauce
1 tablespoon anchovy paste
1 tablespoon salt

1 cup pasteurized egg substitute
10 grinds of pepper
1 cup canola oil
1/4 cup (1 ounce) grated
　　Parmesan cheese

Combine the lemon juice, cider vinegar, Worcestershire sauce, anchovy paste and salt in a blender; process at high speed for 2 minutes. Add the egg substitute and pepper. Add the canola oil gradually, processing constantly to emulsify. Stir in the Parmesan cheese. Store in the refrigerator.

MAKES 2 1/2 CUPS

Hail, Caesar!

This dressing works well on tossed salads, drizzled over sliced flank steak, or on baked potatoes. Spread it on a toasted bun and top with grilled chicken and fresh romaine leaves for a quick chicken Caesar sandwich. Using pasteurized egg substitute in this dressing eliminates the need to cook the egg.

Summertime Fresh Corn Salad

2 ears of fresh corn, cooked
  and cooled
6 cups torn mixed salad greens
1 or 2 tomatoes,
  coarsely chopped
1/2 avocado, cut into
  1/2-inch pieces

1/3 cup thinly sliced red onion
4 to 6 large basil leaves, torn
1/2 cup crumbled blue cheese,
  such as Roquefort, Stilton
  or Danish
Balsamic Lemon Vinaigrette
  (below)

Cut the kernels from the corn cob into a salad bowl using a sharp knife. Add the salad greens, tomatoes, avocado, onion, basil and cheese and toss to combine. Add the Balsamic Lemon Vinaigrette and toss to coat well.

SERVES 6

Balsamic Lemon Vinaigrette

1 tablespoon balsamic vinegar
1 tablespoon fresh lemon juice
5 to 6 teaspoons extra-virgin olive oil
1 teaspoon (heaping) whole grain Dijon mustard
1/2 teaspoon salt
16 to 24 grinds pepper

Combine the balsamic vinegar, lemon juice, olive oil, Dijon mustard, salt and pepper in a jar with a tight-fitting lid and shake to mix well. Store in the refrigerator.

MAKES ABOUT 1/4 CUP

Cranberry and Fennel Salad

4 cups wild field greens
1 head romaine, torn
1 bulb fennel, chopped
1 red onion, sliced
1 cup dried cranberries
1 cup sliced mushrooms
1 cup toasted hazelnuts

1 cup crumbled blue cheese
1 cup canola oil
1/2 cup balsamic vinegar
1 garlic clove, minced
1/2 teaspoon tarragon
1/2 teaspoon cilantro

Combine the wild greens, romaine, fennel, onion, dried cranberries, mushrooms, hazelnuts and blue cheese in a salad bowl.

Mix the canola oil, balsamic vinegar, garlic, tarragon and cilantro in a jar with a tight-fitting lid and shake to mix well. Add the desired amount to the salad and toss to coat evenly.

SERVES 4 TO 6

Cucumber Salad

1 English cucumber, thinly sliced
Salt to taste
1/4 cup rice vinegar
1 tablespoon sugar
1 tablespoon fresh dill weed,
    chopped, or 1 teaspoon
    dried dill weed

1/4 teaspoon salt
1/8 teaspoon pepper
1/2 red bell pepper, thinly sliced
1/4 red onion, thinly sliced

Place the cucumber in a colander over a bowl and sprinkle lightly with salt to taste. Let stand for several minutes.

Combine the rice vinegar, sugar, dill weed, 1/4 teaspoon salt and the pepper in a bowl. Rinse the cucumber slices with cold water and add to the vinegar mixture. Add the bell pepper and onion. Serve chilled or at room temperature. Top with skewers of grilled shrimp for a main-dish salad.

SERVES 4

Cucumber and Fontina Cheese Salad

4 ounces crusty Italian bread
    (about 1/4 loaf)
2 tablespoons olive oil
Salt and pepper to taste
6 cucumbers, peeled
    and chopped
3 tomatoes, chopped

1/2 small red onion, thinly sliced
1/2 cup kalamata olives,
    cut into halves
Cilantro Vinaigrette (below)
1/2 cup (1/2-inch cubes)
    fontina cheese

Preheat the oven to 300 degrees. Cut the bread into 3/4-inch pieces. Spread on a baking sheet and drizzle with the olive oil. Sprinkle with salt and pepper. Bake for 20 minutes or until golden brown, shaking the pan occasionally. Let cool to room temperature.

Combine the cucumbers, tomatoes, onion and olives in a large bowl. Add the Cilantro Vinaigrette, croutons and fontina cheese just before serving; toss to coat evenly.

You can substitute feta cheese for a tangier taste, or use Gruyère, Swiss, Gouda or mozzarella cheese.

SERVES 6

Cilantro Vinaigrette

1/3 cup olive oil
1/4 cup red wine vinegar
1/4 cup chopped fresh cilantro

4 garlic cloves, minced
3/4 teaspoon salt
1/2 teaspoon pepper

Combine the olive oil, red wine vinegar, cilantro, garlic, salt and pepper in a bowl and whisk until smooth.

MAKES ABOUT 3/4 CUP

Holiday Salad with Bacon and Almonds

8 to 10 cups torn romaine and spinach leaves
4 ounces bacon, chopped and crisp-cooked
1 cup sliced mushrooms
1 egg, hard-cooked and sliced or chopped
1/4 cup sliced almonds
Holiday Salad Dressing (below)
1/2 cup (2 ounces) grated Romano cheese
1 red onion, sliced and separated into rings

Combine the salad greens with the bacon in a large bowl. Add the mushrooms, hard-cooked egg and almonds. Add the Holiday Salad Dressing at serving time and top with the Romano cheese and onion rings.

SERVES 8 TO 10

Holiday Salad Dressing

3/4 cup canola oil
1/4 cup white wine vinegar
2 eggs, hard-cooked and mashed
1 teaspoon dry mustard
1/2 teaspoon basil
1 teaspoon salt
1/2 teaspoon pepper

Combine the canola oil, vinegar and eggs in a bowl. Add the dry mustard, basil, salt and pepper and mix well.

MAKES 1 1/2 CUPS

Baby Pea and White Corn Salad

1 (16-ounce) package frozen baby peas
1 (11-ounce) can white Shoe Peg corn, drained, or 1 (10-ounce) package frozen white Shoe Peg corn
1 1/2 cups chopped celery
1 large green bell pepper, chopped
1 cup chopped green onions
1 (4-ounce) jar chopped pimentos, drained
Dill Dressing (below)

Combine the peas, corn, celery, bell pepper, green onions and pimentos in a bowl. Add the Dill Dressing and mix well. Chill for 2 hours or longer, stirring occasionally.

SERVES 6

Dill Dressing

1/2 cup apple cider vinegar
1/4 cup canola oil
1/4 cup sugar
1 teaspoon dried dill weed
1/4 teaspoon salt

Combine the cider vinegar, canola oil, sugar, dill weed and salt in a jar with a tight-fitting lid and shake to mix well.

MAKES 1 CUP

Raspberry Spinach Salad

4 ounces chèvre
1 bunch spinach, trimmed
1 avocado, cut into
    1-inch pieces
1/4 red onion, thinly sliced
5 or 6 mushrooms, thickly sliced

8 to 10 grape tomatoes,
    cut into halves
2 eggs, hard-cooked and sliced
1/2 cup croutons
1/2 cup raspberry vinaigrette

Place the cheese in the freezer for 20 minutes. Combine the spinach with the avocado, onion, mushrooms, tomatoes, eggs and croutons. Pull apart the cheese into small chunks and add to the salad. Add the raspberry vinaigrette and toss to coat evenly. Serve immediately.

SERVES 4 TO 6

Top This!

There are many good toppings for spinach salad. Toasted pine nuts or walnuts add a bit of crunch and smokiness and are also a good gluten-free substitute for croutons. Sliced radishes add crunch and a peppery flavor. Sliced kiwifruit and fresh raspberries or blueberries are great. For a main-dish salad, add sliced cooked chicken or even meat pulled from a commercial rotisserie chicken.

Wilted Spinach and Radicchio Salad with Warm Bacon Dressing

¹/2 head radicchio
1 bunch spinach, trimmed
8 slices thick-cut bacon, cut into
   ¹/2-inch pieces
¹/2 red onion, chopped

1 garlic clove, minced
3 tablespoons cider vinegar
4 eggs, hard-cooked and cut
   into quarters

Cut off the bottom of the radicchio and cut the head into slivers. Combine with the spinach in a large bowl and mix gently.

Cook the bacon in a skillet until crisp. Remove the bacon with a slotted spoon and drain the skillet, reserving 3 tablespoons of the drippings in the skillet. Add the onion to the drippings and sauté for 3 minutes. Stir in the garlic and sauté for 15 seconds. Add the cider vinegar and remove from the heat.

Pour the dressing over the greens in the bowl, scraping the bottom of the skillet to remove any brown bits. Add the bacon to the salad and toss until the greens are coated and slightly wilted.

Spoon onto serving plates and top evenly with the egg quarters. Serve immediately.

This is an excellent way to serve the more bitter greens, such as radicchio, though mâche (lamb's lettuce) and arugula can also be used.

SERVES 6 TO 8

92

Apple and Cabbage Coleslaw

1/2 cup grated apple
1 head cabbage, shredded
1/2 cup half-and-half
1/2 cup mayonnaise

1/2 cup sugar
1/4 cup cider vinegar
1 tablespoon mustard
1/2 teaspoon salt

Combine the apple and cabbage in a large sealable plastic bag. Combine the half-and-half, mayonnaise and sugar in a jar with a tight-fitting lid and shake to dissolve the sugar. Add the cider vinegar, mustard and salt and shake to coat. Add to the cabbage mixture and mix well. Store in the refrigerator.

SERVES 4 TO 6

Marinated Tomato and Mushroom Salad

2 cups olive oil
1 1/2 cups white wine vinegar
2 pounds small fresh
   mushrooms, or large
   mushrooms, cut into quarters
2 teaspoons minced
   green onions
4 cloves garlic, minced
1 teaspoon chopped
   fresh oregano

1 teaspoon chopped fresh basil
2 teaspoons dry mustard
2 teaspoons salt
1 teaspoon pepper
2 small red onions, sliced
1 large green bell pepper, sliced
1 pound cherry tomatoes or
   grape tomatoes, cut into
   halves, or Roma tomatoes,
   chopped

Combine the olive oil, vinegar, mushrooms, green onions, garlic, oregano, basil, dry mustard, salt and pepper in a bowl and mix well. Chill in the refrigerator for 8 hours or longer. Add the onions, bell pepper and tomatoes and toss to mix well. Chill for 4 hours longer.

SERVES 6 TO 8

Jasmine Rice Salad

4 cups water
1 tablespoon vegetable oil
1/2 teaspoon salt
2 cups jasmine rice

1 red bell pepper, chopped
4 green onions, sliced
Rice Wine Vinaigrette (below)

Combine the water, oil and salt in a saucepan and bring to a boil. Add the rice and return to a boil. Reduce the heat to a simmer and cover. Simmer for 15 to 20 minutes or until the liquid is absorbed. Let stand, covered, for 10 minutes. Remove the cover and let cool to room temperature.

Combine the rice with the bell pepper and green onions in a bowl. Add the desired amount of Rice Wine Vinaigrette and toss to coat. Serve chilled or at room temperature.

SERVES 4 TO 6

Rice Wine Vinaigrette

94

3/4 cup vegetable oil
1/2 cup rice vinegar
1/4 cup sesame oil
3 tablespoons soy sauce

2 teaspoons sugar
1 garlic clove, crushed
1 teaspoon grated fresh ginger

Combine the vegetable oil, rice vinegar, sesame oil and soy sauce in a bowl. Add the sugar, garlic and ginger and mix well. Let stand for 30 minutes or longer before serving to develop the flavors.

MAKES 1 3/4 CUPS

Chicken Pistachio Salad

1 1/2 cups shredded cooked chicken breast or rotisserie chicken, chilled
8 cups torn romaine or mixed greens
1/4 cup pistachios
3/4 cup julienned peeled jicama
1/4 cup dried cranberries or fresh pomegranate seeds
Pomegranate Vinaigrette (below)

Combine the chicken with the romaine, pistachios, jicama and cranberries in a large salad bowl. Add the Pomegranate Vinaigrette and toss gently to coat well.

SERVES 4 AS A MAIN DISH OR 8 AS A SIDE DISH

Pomegranate Vinaigrette

1/4 cup balsamic vinegar
1 tablespoon pomegranate molasses
1 tablespoon honey
1 teaspoon Dijon mustard
1 garlic clove, minced
1/4 teaspoon salt
Dash of freshly ground pepper
1/2 cup olive oil (not extra-virgin) or grapeseed oil

Combine the balsamic vinegar, pomegranate molasses, honey, Dijon mustard, garlic, salt and pepper in a bowl and whisk to mix well. Drizzle in the olive oil, whisking constantly until the mixture emulsifies and thickens slightly. You can also process the mixture in the same manner in a food processor or blender.

MAKES ABOUT 3/4 CUP

Smoked Salmon Cobb Salad

1/2 head red leaf lettuce
1/2 head romaine
2 tomatoes, chopped
8 ounces smoked salmon, chopped
6 slices bacon, crisp-cooked and crumbled
3 eggs, hard-cooked and chopped

1/2 cup crumbled Roquefort cheese
1 avocado, chopped
2 tablespoons chopped fresh chives
2 tablespoons chopped fresh parsley
3/4 cup Dijon Dressing (below)

Line the bottom of a deep serving platter with the red leaf lettuce and romaine. Arrange the tomatoes in a row down the center of the platter. Arrange the salmon, bacon, eggs and cheese in rows on either side of the tomatoes.

Sprinkle the avocado around the edge of the platter and sprinkle the salad with chives and parsley. Whisk the Dijon Dressing to mix well and drizzle over the salad.

SERVES 6

Dijon Dressing

1 tablespoon Dijon mustard
1/4 teaspoon sugar
1/4 cup balsamic vinegar
3/4 teaspoon Worcestershire sauce

1 small garlic clove, minced
1/4 teaspoon salt
Freshly ground pepper to taste
2/3 cup olive oil
Juice of 1/2 lemon

Combine the Dijon mustard, sugar, balsamic vinegar, Worcestershire sauce, garlic, salt and pepper in a jar with a tight-fitting lid and shake to mix well. Add the olive oil and lemon juice and shake until emulsified. Chill until serving time.

MAKES ABOUT 1 CUP

Sesame Crab Salad

8 ounces crab meat
1/4 cup lemon juice
1 to 2 tablespoons toasted
    sesame oil, or to taste
1 shallot, thinly sliced
2 tablespoons chopped cilantro

Grated zest of 1 lemon
Pinch of cayenne pepper or
    Tabasco sauce, or to taste
1 avocado, sliced
1 cup julienned daikon radishes

Combine the crab meat, lemon juice, sesame oil, shallot, cilantro, lemon zest and cayenne pepper in a bowl and mix gently. Arrange the avocado and radishes on two serving plates. Top with the crab salad and garnish with toasted sesame seeds.

SERVES 2

Washington State Capitol Campus

Positioned prominently over the capital city of Olympia, Washington State's Capitol building, completed in 1928, serves as a working governmental center. Arguably the most impressive structure in the state, it is the fourth-tallest masonry dome in the world and the last great domed building to be built in the United States. Lavishly surrounded by gardens, memorials, a fountain patterned after the Tivoli Fountain in Copenhagen, Denmark, and a lake designed to reflect the Capitol building, visitors will find themselves immersed in the history and beauty of the Washington State Capitol campus.

Entrées

ENTRÉES

◀ HEARTY SLOW-COOKED LAMB WITH
MUSHROOM SAUCE AND RIGATONI

Beef Bourguignon

3 slices bacon, chopped
2 pounds lean beef sirloin,
    trimmed and cut into
    1/2×4-inch strips
1 garlic clove, minced
16 ounces mushrooms, sliced
1 bay leaf, crushed
1 tablespoon minced
    fresh parsley

1/2 teaspoon dried thyme
1/2 teaspoon salt
1/8 teaspoon cracked pepper
1/4 cup (1/2 stick) butter
1/4 cup all-purpose flour
1 (14-ounce) can
    beef consommé
1 cup burgundy or merlot
Hot cooked egg noodles or rice

Cook the bacon in a heavy saucepan or Dutch oven until crisp. Remove with a slotted spoon, reserving the drippings in the saucepan. Add the beef to the drippings and sauté until evenly browned. Add the garlic, mushrooms, bay leaf, parsley, thyme, salt and pepper. Return the bacon to the saucepan and mix well. Remove from the heat.

Melt the butter in a medium saucepan. Add the flour and cook until the flour begins to brown, stirring constantly. Add the consommé and wine and cook until slightly thickened, stirring constantly. Add to the beef mixture. Simmer, covered, for 1 1/2 hours or until the beef is tender. Serve over egg noodles or rice.

SERVES 6

Inspiring

It is difficult for foster children to make it all the way through high school. With all the daily challenges they face, they may find school too overwhelming to complete. The Junior League of Olympia (JLO) is committed to encouraging and supporting foster youth at this possible turning point in their lives. JLO celebrates **graduating foster care children** by providing them the essential household items to start lives on their own. JLO also established a **Junior League of Olympia Legacy Scholarship** to financially assist a local student annually.

1 1/2 teaspoons kosher salt
1/2 teaspoon ground cumin
1/2 teaspoon coriander
1/4 teaspoon pepper
1 flank steak
Chimichurri Sauce (below)

Combine the kosher salt, cumin, coriander and pepper. Rub over the surface of the steak. Let stand for 30 minutes or longer.

Preheat a grill and place the steak on the grill. Grill just until medium-rare. Slice diagonally across the grain and spoon Chimichurri Sauce over the slices. Serve with rice and salad.

SERVES 4

2 garlic cloves
1 1/2 cups cilantro
1/2 cup Italian parsley
1/4 cup vinegar
1/3 cup olive oil
1/4 teaspoon cayenne pepper

Chimichurri Sauce

Combine the garlic, cilantro, parsley, vinegar, olive oil and cayenne pepper in a food processor in the order listed. Process until smooth.

MAKES ABOUT 2 CUPS

Blackened Tri-Tip Steak

1 (3- to 5-pound) tri-tip
   beef steak
2 to 3 tablespoons Steak Rub
   (below)
1 ounce (2 tablespoons)
   Kentucky bourbon

1/4 cup olive oil
1/4 teaspoon balsamic vinegar
1/2 teaspoon honey
6 garlic cloves, minced
Pinch of dried rosemary

Place the steak in a large sealable plastic bag. Add the Steak Rub, shaking to coat well. Seal the bag and let stand in the refrigerator for 1 to 24 hours.

Combine the bourbon, olive oil, balsamic vinegar, honey, garlic and rosemary in a small bowl and mix well. Add to the steak. Seal the bag and marinate at room temperature for 30 minutes.

Preheat the grill to hot. Add the steak and sear on one side. Reduce the heat and turn the steak over. Grill until done to taste. Place on a platter and slice across the grain to serve.

SERVES 8

Steak Rub

2 1/2 tablespoons paprika
2 tablespoons garlic powder
1 tablespoon onion powder
1 tablespoon dried oregano
1 tablespoon dried thyme

2 tablespoons salt
1 tablespoon black pepper
1 teaspoon cayenne pepper,
   or to taste

Combine the paprika, garlic powder, onion powder, oregano, thyme, salt, black pepper and cayenne pepper in a bowl; mix well. Store in an airtight container.

MAKES 3/4 CUP

1 pound lean ground beef
1 pound bacon, crisp-cooked and crumbled
1 onion, chopped
1 (15-ounce) can kidney beans, drained and rinsed
1 (15-ounce) can butter beans, drained and rinsed

1 (31-ounce) can pork and beans
1/2 cup packed brown sugar
1/2 cup ketchup
2 tablespoons vinegar
1 teaspoon liquid smoke
1/2 teaspoon dry mustard

Sauté the ground beef in a saucepan, stirring until brown and crumbly; drain. Combine with the bacon, onion, kidney beans, butter beans and pork and beans in a bowl and mix well. Add the brown sugar, ketchup, vinegar, liquid smoke and dry mustard; mix well.

Spoon the mixture into a slow cooker and cook on Low for 3 hours or longer.

SERVES 10 TO 12

---

2 pounds ground round
1 pound hot or mild bulk pork sausage
1 1/2 cups cornflakes, crushed
1 egg
1 (10-ounce) package frozen spinach, thawed and drained

1 cup chopped onion
1 cup (4 ounces) grated Parmesan cheese
3 tablespoons chopped parsley
1 cup burgundy, or 1/4 cup Worcestershire sauce
Salt and pepper to taste

Preheat the oven to 350 degrees. Combine the ground round and sausage in a bowl and mix well. Add the cornflakes, egg, spinach, onion, cheese, parsley, wine, salt and pepper and mix well.

Press the mixture into a 5×9-inch loaf pan. Bake for 1 hour. Remove to a serving plate and slice to serve.

SERVES 8

Hearty Slow-Cooked Lamb with Mushroom Sauce and Rigatoni

1 tablespoon olive oil

2 pounds lamb shoulder arm chops, trimmed and cut into 3 pieces

1 teaspoon kosher salt, or to taste

1/4 teaspoon coarsely ground pepper

1/2 cup chopped onion

1 1/2 cups sliced mushrooms

1 tablespoon minced fresh garlic

1/3 cup tomato paste

2 teaspoons grated orange zest

1/8 teaspoon crushed red pepper flakes

2 tablespoons balsamic vinegar

1/2 cup red wine

1 cup canned low-sodium beef broth

3 fresh sage leaves

Hot cooked rigatoni

Olive oil for drizzling

2 ounces soft chèvre

Heat 1 tablespoon olive oil in a large nonstick saucepan over medium-high heat. Season the lamb chops on both sides with 1 teaspoon kosher salt and the pepper. Add to the saucepan half at a time and sauté for 1 1/2 to 2 minutes or until brown; remove to a slow cooker.

Add the onion and mushrooms to the saucepan and sauté for 4 minutes or until brown, stirring frequently. Stir in the garlic, tomato paste, orange zest and red pepper flakes. Cook for 2 minutes. Whisk in the balsamic vinegar and wine. Cook for 2 minutes.

Stir in the broth and sage leaves. Bring to a boil and pour over the lamb, scraping up the browned bits from the saucepan. Cook on High for 6 hours or on Low for 8 to 10 hours. Turn off the slow cooker. Remove and discard the lamb bones. Shred the meat into the sauce. Let stand, covered, for several minutes. Serve over rigatoni drizzled with olive oil. Crumble the chèvre over the top; garnish with fresh sage leaves.

SERVES 6

Chef Kathy Casey

We're all busy and sometimes we just need to load up that slow cooker and head out the door. Plus, you come back to a house that smells so good! Tender chunks of lamb, a touch of orange peel, balsamic vinegar, onion and garlic, mushrooms, tomato paste, red wine, and fresh sage meld into a robust meat sauce. Chef Kathy Casey suggests adding a fresh arugula salad, crusty bread, and a glass of red wine to round out a meal. What more could you ask to come home to?

Luscious Lamb Chops

1/2 cup fresh lemon juice
1 large garlic clove, crushed
1 tablespoon fresh rosemary

1/2 teaspoon salt
1/4 teaspoon pepper
4 thick lamb chops

Mix the first five ingredients in a shallow dish. Add the lamb chops, turning to coat. Marinate for 30 to 60 minutes. Preheat a grill. Add the lamb chops and grill to the desired degree of doneness.

SERVES 4

Carnitas

5 pounds pork butt or
    pork shoulder
2 cups orange juice with pulp
1 (12-ounce) can regular beer
3 jalapeño chiles, seeded and
    chopped, or to taste

2 onions, chopped
6 garlic cloves, crushed
1 tablespoon ground cumin
2 teaspoons dried oregano
Salt and pepper to taste

Cut the pork into 3-inch pieces. Combine with the orange juice, beer, chiles, onions, garlic, cumin, oregano, salt and pepper in a large Dutch oven. Add enough water to just cover the meat. Bring to a boil over high heat. Cover and reduce the heat to medium-low. Simmer for 2 to 3 hours or until the pork is very tender.

Remove the pork to a cutting board and let cool slightly. Drain and discard the cooking liquid, reserving the vegetables. Shred the pork with two forks, trimming and discarding the visible fat.

Preheat the oven to 375 degrees. Combine the pork and vegetables in the Dutch oven and mix well. Season with salt and pepper. Bake, uncovered, for 45 minutes, or until the edges of the pork just begin to become brown and crisp, stirring twice. Serve with warm corn tortillas, shredded Cotija or ranchero cheese, guacamole and salsa.

SERVES 8

Suggested Wine Pairing: Campo Viejo Reserva, Rioja, Spain,
100% Tempranillo

Pork with Cherry Port Sauce

1/2 cup dried cherries
1/2 cup (or more) port
1 (1-pound) pork tenderloin
Salt and pepper to taste
1/4 cup vegetable oil

2 tablespoons chopped onion
1 garlic clove, chopped
1 tablespoon balsamic vinegar
1 teaspoon sugar

Combine the dried cherries with the wine in a small bowl and let stand for 30 minutes.

Preheat the oven to 400 degrees. Sprinkle the pork with salt and pepper. Sear in the heated vegetable oil in an ovenproof skillet for 3 to 5 minutes. Place in the oven and roast for 15 minutes. Let stand at room temperature for 5 to 10 minutes. Slice into medallions.

Add the onion and garlic to the drippings in the skillet and sauté until tender. Add the cherry mixture, balsamic vinegar and sugar and mix well. Cook until reduced by one-half, adding additional wine if needed. Place the pork medallions on serving plates and top with the sauce.

SERVES 2 OR 3

Suggested Wine Pairing: Mark West Pinot Noir, California

106

Reprinted with permission of
The Olympian/Tony Overman

Mt. Rainier

The sight of Mt. Rainier from Olympia is truly breathtaking. Mt. Rainier, a volcano covered with miles of snow and glacial ice, dominates the Cascade Range. The Mountain, as it is referred to by locals, is surrounded by diverse wildlife habitats, subalpine meadows with an amazing array of wildflowers, and lush old-growth trees.

Pork Tenderloin with Spiced Bourbon Marinade

1/4 cup Kentucky bourbon
1/4 cup soy sauce
1/4 cup vegetable oil
1/4 cup packed brown sugar
1/4 cup Dijon mustard

3 garlic cloves, minced
1 teaspoon minced fresh ginger
1 teaspoon Worcestershire sauce
2 (1-pound) pork tenderloins

Combine the bourbon, soy sauce, oil, brown sugar, Dijon mustard, garlic, ginger and Worcestershire sauce in a bowl; whisk until smooth. Pour into a sealable plastic bag and add the pork, turning to coat. Marinate in the refrigerator for 8 hours or longer.

Preheat a charcoal grill to hot. Drain the pork and discard the marinade. Place the pork on the grill and grill for 15 to 25 minutes or to 165 degrees on a meat thermometer; do not overcook.

Cut the pork into 1/2-inch slices to serve as a main dish, or into 1/4-inch slices for sandwiches. You can also broil the pork 6 inches from the heat source for 16 to 18 minutes.

SERVES 6

Olympia Wooden Boat Festival

Each year Olympia celebrates its rich history and tradition of wooden boats during the four-day Wooden Boat Festival. Enthusiasts come from near and far to view wooden boats of all conditions, vintages, and sizes throughout Percival Landing Park, one of Olympia's three waterfront parks. Puget Sound offers not only some of the best cruising grounds in the world, but also a climate that is easy on the old wooden classics. A fun family tradition offered at the festival is the Children's Boat-Building Booth, where children are encouraged to use their imaginations to build their own wooden boats.

Reprinted with permission of
The Olympian/Toni Bailey

Stuffed Pork Tenderloin with Apple Brandy Cream Sauce

3 (1-pound) pork tenderloins, trimmed

6 ounces Emmentaler cheese, sliced 1/4 inch thick

2 Granny Smith apples, peeled and sliced 1/4-inch thick

4 ounces goat cheese, sliced 1/4 inch thick

Olive oil

Salt and pepper to taste

Apple Brandy Cream Sauce (page 109)

Pound the pork 1/4 inch thick between plastic wrap, maintaining a rectangular shape. Wrap in the plastic wrap and chill in the refrigerator.

Place the pork on a work surface and arrange the Emmentaler cheese slices end to end across the tenderloins about 3 inches from the bottom edge. Arrange the apple slices over the cheese and layer the goat cheese on top. Fold and roll the pork tightly to enclose the stuffing, folding in the ends. Secure the rolls with butcher's twine. Coat with olive oil and season with salt and pepper. Chill in the refrigerator.

Preheat the oven to 400 degrees. Sear the pork on all sides and both ends in a hot ovenproof skillet. Place in the oven and roast for 25 minutes or to an internal temperature for 145 to 150 degrees. Remove and cover with a towel or foil tent and let stand for 10 minutes.

Remove the twine and cut the tenderloins into 1/4- to 1/3-inch slices. Top each serving with 2 to 4 tablespoons Apple Brandy Cream Sauce.

SERVES 8 TO 10

Chef John Edwards

Pacific Northwest chef John Edwards ties the pork tenderloins to help them cook evenly, to make them more visually pleasing, and to create more uniform slices when they are carved. The key to tying a pork tenderloin is to use butcher's twine or kitchen twine, available at most markets in the kitchen aisle. Make simple knots at about one-inch intervals down the length of the tenderloin, being careful to tie it just snugly enough that it won't unroll and lose the stuffing.

Apple Brandy Cream Sauce

1/2 Granny Smith apple, chopped
2 tablespoons chopped shallots
4 ounces (1/2 cup) brandy

2 cups heavy cream
2 ounces Emmentaler cheese
Salt and pepper to taste

Sauté the apple and shallots in the brandy in a shallow sauté pan until most of the liquid has evaporated. Add the cream and cook until reduced by half. Add the Emmentaler cheese and cook until slightly thickened. Season with salt and pepper and add additional brandy, if desired.

MAKES ABOUT 1 CUP

Pork Tenderloin Medallions with Balsamic Rosemary Sauce

1 pork tenderloin
Salt and pepper taste
2 tablespoons porcini oil or other flavorful oil
8 ounces sliced bacon
1/4 cup olive oil

2 garlic cloves, chopped
1 large shallot, chopped
1/3 cup balsamic vinegar
2 tablespoons molasses
1 sprig fresh rosemary

Preheat the oven to 400 degrees. Season the pork with salt and pepper. Sear in the heated porcini oil in an ovenproof skillet for 3 to 5 minutes or until brown on all sides. Place in the oven and roast for 15 minutes. Let stand for 5 to 10 minutes.

Cook the bacon in a sauté pan. Drain, reserving 1/4 cup drippings in the pan; stir in the olive oil. Add the garlic and shallot and sauté until tender. Add the balsamic vinegar, molasses and rosemary. Bring to a boil and cook until reduced to the desired consistency.

Cut the pork into medallions and drizzle with half the sauce. Reserve the remaining sauce to use as a salad dressing. Crumble the bacon and sprinkle over the pork.

SERVES 2 TO 3

Fried Rice with Pork and Thai Basil

3 tablespoons canola oil
3 garlic cloves, minced
1/2 to 1 cup chopped sweet
onion or yellow onion
1 red chile, seeded
and julienned
1 to 2 cups Thai basil or
sweet basil
1 cup sliced pork tenderloin or
pork belly

4 eggs, beaten
3 cups steamed jasmine
rice, cooled
1 tablespoon light soy sauce
1 tablespoon fish sauce
1/4 cup diagonally-sliced
scallions
4 lime wedges
Spicy Fish Sauce (below)

Heat the canola oil in a skillet or wok over high heat. Add the garlic and stir-fry until golden brown. Add the onion, chile and basil and stir-fry until fragrant. Add the pork and stir-fry until cooked through.

Stir the pork mixture to the side of the skillet and pour the eggs in the center. Cook for 2 seconds, stirring vigorously. Stir in the rice, soy sauce, fish sauce and scallions. Stir-fry until well mixed and heated through. Serve with the lime wedges and Spicy Fish Sauce.

SERVES 4

Spicy Fish Sauce (*Prik Nam Pla*)

Cooks in Thailand use Spicy Fish Sauce as we use salt and pepper for seasoning. To prepare it, combine 1/4 cup fish sauce with 2 sliced Thai or jalapeño chiles and 1/2 teaspoon sugar in a small bowl. Mix to dissolve the sugar. Place one sliced lime in the center. This makes about one-half cup of sauce.

Chicken Paprikash

1/2 cup chopped onion
1/4 cup vegetable oil
2 garlic cloves, minced
1 tablespoon Hungarian
   paprika
3 pounds chicken pieces
Salt to taste

1 tomato, finely chopped
1 cup chopped green
   bell pepper
1/2 cup chicken broth or water
11/4 cups sour cream
1/4 cup all-purpose flour
Pepper to taste

Sauté the onion in the oil in a large skillet over medium heat for 5 minutes or until translucent. Reduce the heat to medium-low and add the garlic and paprika. Cook for 30 seconds, stirring constantly. Add the chicken and salt. Sauté until the chicken is brown. Stir in the broth.

Simmer, covered, for 20 minutes or until the chicken is nearly tender. Add the tomato and bell pepper and simmer for 15 minutes longer or until the chicken is cooked through. Remove the chicken to a platter and cover with foil.

Blend the sour cream and flour in a small bowl. Add to the sauce in the skillet and cook until thickened, whisking constantly. Return the chicken to the skillet, turning to coat evenly with the sauce. Season with salt and pepper. Serve with small pasta or dumplings.

SERVES 4

Coconut Chicken

2 to 3 cups finely grated
   unsweetened coconut
1 teaspoon salt
1/2 teaspoon cracked pepper
1 cup all-purpose flour

2 teaspoons dried basil
4 boneless skinless
   chicken breasts
1 cup Dijon mustard
3 eggs, beaten

Preheat the oven to 450 degrees. Toss the coconut with the salt and pepper on a plate. Mix the flour with the basil on a plate. Pound the chicken between plastic wrap until thin. Spread each chicken breast with Dijon mustard and then coat with the flour mixture. Dip into the eggs and coat with the coconut.

Arrange the chicken on a greased baking sheet and spray with nonstick cooking spray. Bake for 15 minutes or until cooked through.

SERVES 4

Grilled Chicken with Tarragon

1/4 cup Dijon mustard
1/4 cup dry white wine
1 tablespoon olive oil
1 tablespoon honey
1/3 cup fresh tarragon

1/2 teaspoon thyme
2 tablespoons grated onion
1 garlic clove, minced
1 teaspoon brown sugar
4 chicken breasts

Preheat a grill to low heat. Mix the Dijon mustard, wine, olive oil and honey in a bowl. Stir in the tarragon, thyme, onion, garlic and brown sugar. Brush some of the sauce on the chicken. Place the chicken on the grill and grill until the juices run clear, brushing frequently with the remaining sauce.

SERVES 4

Dried Herbs

Remember that dried herbs are three times more potent than fresh herbs, so if your recipe calls for three teaspoons (one tablespoon) of a fresh herb, reduce the measure to one teaspoon, or one-third of that, for a dried herb.

2 tablespoons soy sauce
2 tablespoons fish sauce
1/2 cup fresh basil or purple
    Thai basil
1/2 cup fresh mint
1/2 cup fresh cilantro
1/4 cup chopped fresh ginger
5 garlic cloves
2 tablespoons brown sugar

1 serrano chile
1 cup unsweetened
    coconut milk
8 boneless skinless
    chicken breasts
8 hamburger buns or
    Kaiser rolls
Ginger-Lime Aïoli (below)
8 leaves butter lettuce

Grilled Thai Chicken Sandwiches with Ginger-Lime Aïoli

Combine the soy sauce, fish sauce, basil, mint, cilantro, ginger, garlic, brown sugar and chile in a food processor and process until blended, scraping the bowl frequently. Add the coconut milk and process until smooth.

Combine the marinade with the chicken in a sealable plastic bag and mix well. Marinate in the refrigerator for 8 to 14 hours, turning the bag occasionally.

Preheat a grill to medium heat. Drain the chicken, discarding the marinade. Grill until cooked through, taking care not to char.

Split the buns and spread 2 tablespoons Ginger-Lime Aïoli on each roll. Top each roll bottom with a piece of chicken and a lettuce leaf and replace the roll tops.

SERVES 8

1 cup mayonnaise
1/2 cup chopped fresh cilantro
3 tablespoons fresh lime juice

1 tablespoon grated fresh ginger
1 teaspoon sriracha sauce or
    chili-garlic paste, or to taste

Ginger-Lime Aïoli

Combine the mayonnaise, cilantro, lime juice, ginger and sriracha sauce in a food processor or mixing bowl. Process or mix with a hand mixer until smooth. Spoon into a bowl and chill until serving time.

MAKES 1 1/2 CUPS

Chanterelle Mushroom Chicken

1 cup all-purpose flour
1 tablespoon dried oregano
Freshly cracked pepper to taste
4 to 6 chicken thighs with skin
2 tablespoons vegetable oil

8 to 12 chanterelle mushrooms,
    cut into bite-size pieces
1/2 cup chicken broth
1 1/2 cups sherry

Mix the flour, oregano and pepper together in a bowl. Add the chicken and toss to coat. Cook the chicken, covered, in the oil in a skillet over medium-high heat for 25 to 30 minutes or until golden brown, turning every 5 minutes. Drain on paper towels.

Drain the skillet, reserving 1 tablespoon of the drippings. Add the mushrooms to the drippings and sauté for 5 minutes. Add the broth and chicken to the skillet. Cook, loosely covered, until the chicken broth is reduced by half.

Add half the wine and cook, loosely covered, until reduced by half. Add the remaining wine and cook until reduced to the desired consistency. Serve with mashed potatoes for a hearty fall meal.

SERVES 4

Suggested Wine Pairing: Bodegas Borsao, Borsao, Spain, Garnacha & Tempranillo

Hot Chicken and Cheese Heroes

2 cups chopped cooked chicken
1 1/2 cups chopped celery
1/2 cup mayonnaise
1/4 cup slivered almonds, toasted
1 tablespoon grated onion

1 tablespoon lemon juice
1 teaspoon salt
1/8 teaspoon pepper
4 large French rolls
1 cup (4 ounces) shredded Cheddar cheese

Combine the chicken, celery, mayonnaise, almonds, onion, lemon juice, salt and pepper in a bowl. Cut off the tops of the rolls and scoop out the centers. Fill the rolls with the chicken mixture and wrap with plastic wrap. Chill in the refrigerator.

Preheat the oven to 375 degrees. Unwrap the rolls and place on a baking sheet; sprinkle with the cheese. Let stand for 30 minutes. Bake for 25 minutes or until the cheese is bubbly.

SERVES 4

Olympia, the Jewel of South Puget Sound

There's much more than politics taking place in Washington's capital city. Picturesque and quaint, the town is nestled among the dramatic Olympic Mountains, Mt. Rainier, and the waters at the southern end of the Puget Sound. It boasts intriguing arts and festivals, creative restaurants and coffee houses, an award-winning children's museum, and Washington's second-largest farmer's market. The beautiful Capitol campus gives Olympia a distinctively elegant feel and lively pace during the legislative session.

Game Hens with Vermouth Marinade

6 Cornish game hens
Fresh parsley
Fresh tarragon
Vermouth Marinade (below)
Onion powder to taste

1 teaspoon dried tarragon, or
   2 teaspoons fresh tarragon
Salt to taste
Fresh watercress (optional)

Stuff the game hens with parsley and fresh tarragon. Combine with the Vermouth Marinade in a baking dish and sprinkle lightly with onion powder. Turn the hens breast side down and crumble 1/2 teaspoon of the dried tarragon over the top. Marinate in the refrigerator for 8 to 24 hours.

Preheat the oven to 400 degrees. Roast the hens for 30 minutes. Turn the hens breast side up and sprinkle with the remaining 1/2 teaspoon dried tarragon. Roast for 30 minutes longer, basting frequently with the pan juices. Remove the herbs from the cavities and baste again. Season with salt and stuff the cavities again with additional fresh tarragon, parsley and/or watercress. Serve warm or at room temperature. You can also skewer the hens and grill on a rotisserie.

SERVES 6

Suggested Wine Pairing: Famega Vinho Verde, Portugal

Vermouth Marinade

1/2 cup olive oil
1/2 cup soy sauce
1/2 cup lemon juice
1/2 cup dry vermouth

4 garlic cloves, crushed
1 tablespoon salt
Cracked pepper to taste

Combine the olive oil, soy sauce, lemon juice, wine, garlic, salt and pepper in a bowl and mix well.

MAKES 2 CUPS

Sesame Noodles

12 ounces Chinese egg noodles
1 teaspoon sesame oil
3 1/2 tablespoons soy sauce
2 tablespoons rice vinegar
2 tablespoons tahini
2 tablespoons sesame oil
1 tablespoon creamy
    peanut butter
1 tablespoon sugar

1 tablespoon grated fresh ginger
4 garlic cloves, minced
2 teaspoons chili-garlic paste,
    or to taste
1 carrot, shredded
1/2 English cucumber, peeled
    and cut into thin 2-inch sticks
1/4 cup chopped roasted peanuts

Cook the noodles in boiling water in a large saucepan for 5 to 7 minutes or until tender. Drain the noodles, rinse with cold water and drain again. Toss with 1 teaspoon sesame oil in a bowl.

Combine the soy sauce, rice vinegar, tahini, 2 tablespoons sesame oil, the peanut butter, sugar, ginger, garlic and chili-garlic paste in a bowl; whisk to mix well.

Add the noodles to the soy sauce mixture and toss to coat evenly. Spoon into a serving bowl and top with the carrot, cucumber and peanuts. Serve at room temperature.

SERVES 4 TO 6

117

Noodle Notions

You can turn this meatless take-out classic into a simple meal by adding thinly-sliced grilled flank steak, chicken breast, or prawns and serving it with stir-fried vegetables. For a quick stir-fry, use packaged shredded broccoli slaw, green onions, and a sliced bell pepper.

Prosciutto and Goat Cheese Pizza with Rosemary

1 tablespoon olive oil
1 cup thinly sliced onion
Pinch each of sugar and salt
1/2 cup (2 ounces) shredded Swiss cheese
1 Rustic Pizza Crust (page 119), prebaked for
    4 minutes on each side
8 slices prosciutto
4 ounces chilled chèvre or other goat cheese, crumbled
Leaves of 1 stem fresh rosemary

Preheat the oven to 500 degrees. Place a pizza stone in the oven and heat for 20 minutes.

Heat the olive oil in a sauté pan over medium-low heat. Add the onion, sugar and salt. Cook for 45 minutes or until the onion is golden brown and caramelized, stirring occasionally.

Sprinkle a thin layer of the Swiss cheese all the way to the edge of the Rustic Pizza Crust. Layer with the caramelized onion and prosciutto to the edge of the crust. Crumble the goat cheese over the prosciutto and top with the rosemary.

Slide the pizza and baking parchment onto the heated pizza stone and bake for 5 minutes or until bubbly and done to taste. Cut into wedges to serve.

SERVES 4

Pizza Pointers

- Many pizza lovers do not use tomato sauce on their pizzas, as many sauces can make the crust soggy. The same is true for fresh mozzarella.
- Bake the pizza dough on a preheated pizza stone for 5 minutes on each side before topping it.
- For a regular crust, top the pizza and bake on a heated pizza stone for 10 to 15 minutes or until the toppings are heated through and the crust is golden brown. For a thin crust, let the dough rise for 20 minutes, then press to remove the air and flatten the crust before topping it. For a firm crust with a bit of crusty edge, prebake the crust for 4 minutes on each side before topping it.

Portobello and Gorgonzola Cheese Pizza with Arugula

2 large portobello
 mushroom caps, chopped
1 tablespoon olive oil
1/2 cup (2 ounces) shredded
 Swiss cheese
1/2 cup crumbled
 Gorgonzola cheese

1 Rustic Pizza Crust (below),
 prebaked for 4 minutes on
 each side
1 cup fresh arugula
Olive oil for drizzling

Preheat the oven to 500 degrees. Place a pizza stone in the oven and heat for 20 minutes.

Sauté the mushrooms in the olive oil in a sauté pan for 10 minutes or until tender. Layer the Swiss cheese, mushrooms and Gorgonzola cheese on the Rustic Pizza Crust.

Slide the pizza and baking parchment onto the heated pizza stone and bake for 5 minutes or until heated through. Top with the arugula and drizzle with additional olive oil. Cut into wedges to serve.

SERVES 4

Rustic Pizza Crust

1 envelope dry yeast
1/4 teaspoon sugar
1 1/2 cups warm water
1 tablespoon olive oil

3 1/4 cups all-purpose flour, or
 2 1/4 cups all-purpose flour
 and 1 cup whole wheat flour
1 1/2 teaspoons salt

Combine the yeast and sugar with the warm water in a large bowl. Let stand for 5 minutes. Stir in the olive oil. Mix the flour and salt in a bowl. Add to the yeast mixture and mix well. Knead by hand on a floured surface or with a bread hook in a bowl for 6 to 8 minutes or until smooth and elastic. Cover with plastic wrap and let rise for 45 minutes. Spread into a circle on baking parchment. Top and bake using the recipe directions.

MAKES 1 CRUST

Fish & Shellfish

FISH & SHELLFISH

◀ SOUTH SOUND STEAMER CLAMS

Pecan and Avocado-Crusted Halibut

1 cup pecans
1 small garlic clove, minced
Juice of 1 lime or lemon
1 teaspoon salt
1 teaspoon pepper
1 ripe avocado, mashed

1 teaspoon olive oil (optional)
1 cup finely chopped cilantro
4 (1-inch-thick) halibut steaks
    with skin (6 to 8 ounces
    each), chilled
Rock salt or kosher salt

Preheat the oven to 300 degrees. Spread the pecans on a baking sheet. Toast for 10 minutes, tossing occasionally and checking closely to avoid burning. Let cool and then cut into pieces the size of rice grains. Increase the oven temperature to 400 degrees.

Combine the garlic, lime juice, salt and pepper in a deep bowl or food processor. Add the avocado and mix until smooth, adding the olive oil if needed for the desired consistency. Reserve 1 tablespoon of the cilantro and add the remaining cilantro to the avocado mixture.

Spread the mixture thinly over the top and sides of each halibut steak; the coating should be just thick enough to help the pecans adhere to the fish and may not require the entire amount. Roll the halibut in the pecans in a plate, pressing to adhere.

Sprinkle rock salt to a depth of 1/8- to 1/4-inch in an ovenproof skillet or shallow roasting pan. Cover the salt with foil. The pan should be just large enough to hold the halibut with room for air circulation around them; the insulated pan will allow the halibut to cook from the top rather than from the surface of the pan. You can also use a cedar plank.

Roast the halibut skin side down for 15 minutes or just until slightly firm and some opaque juices can be seen coming through the crust; it will continue to cook after it is removed from the oven.

Remove from the foil, leaving the skin on the foil if possible. Sprinkle with the reserved cilantro and serve with lime or lemon wedges.

SERVES 4

Grilled Halibut with Blueberry Mint Salsa

1¹/2 pounds halibut fillets, cut
　　into 4 servings
Salt and pepper to taste

Blueberry Mint Salsa (below)
4 sprigs fresh mint

Preheat a charcoal grill. Season the halibut with salt and pepper. Place on the grill and sear for 4 to 5 minutes on each side or until opaque, turning once.

Place the Blueberry Salsa in a saucepan and heat over very low heat until heated through. Place the halibut fillets on four serving plates and spoon Blueberry Salsa over the top. Top each serving with a sprig of fresh mint.

SERVES 4

Blueberry Mint Salsa

1 cup blueberries
1 cup finely chopped mixed red
　　and yellow bell peppers
2 small green onions,
　　finely chopped
2 tablespoons chopped
　　fresh cilantro

¹/4 cup chopped fresh mint
1 tablespoon finely chopped
　　poblano chile
1 tablespoon red wine vinegar
Juice of 2 limes
Juice of 1 lemon

Combine the blueberries with the bell peppers, green onions, cilantro, mint, poblano chile, red wine vinegar, lime juice and lemon juice in a small bowl; mix well. Chill for 2 to 3 hours to develop the flavors.

SERVES 4

Healthful Halibut

This recipe showcases the fabulous halibut that is caught off the Washington Coast. Halibut is a lean, mild white fish that lends itself well to fresh light flavors like this salsa. The colorful, nutrient-packed salsa is also great with any grilled seafood or chicken.

Spicy Saucy Halibut

2 pounds halibut, snapper,
   sea bass or rockfish fillets
1 tablespoon extra-virgin olive oil
Salt and black pepper to taste
1 tablespoon extra-virgin olive oil
3 garlic cloves, minced
1 (28-ounce) can
   diced tomatoes

$1/2$ cup kalamata olives,
   cut into halves
3 tablespoons fresh basil,
   thinly sliced
$1 1/2$ tablespoons rinsed
   drained capers
$1/2$ teaspoon crushed red
   pepper flakes, or to taste

Preheat the oven to 350 degrees. Pat the halibut dry with a paper towel and place skin side down in a glass baking dish. Drizzle with 1 tablespoon olive oil and season with salt and black pepper. Bake for 15 to 18 minutes or just until cooked through.

Heat 1 tablespoon olive oil in a 12-inch skillet over medium-low heat. Add the garlic and sauté for 1 minute, taking care not to brown the garlic. Add the remaining ingredients. Increase the heat to medium and simmer for 10 minutes.

Cut the halibut into serving portions and lift gently with a spatula to a serving platter, leaving the skin in the baking dish. Spoon the sauce over the halibut. Serve on pasta, if desired.

SERVES 4 TO 6

Mexican Fish Fillets

1 pound firm white fish fillets
$1/2$ cup (2 ounces) shredded
   Monterey Jack cheese
$1/2$ cup salsa

2 tablespoons mayonnaise
1 teaspoon fresh lime juice
$1/2$ teaspoon pepper

Preheat the oven to 400 degrees. Arrange the fish in a baking dish sprayed with nonstick cooking spray. Combine the cheese, salsa, mayonnaise, lime juice and pepper in a bowl and mix well. Spread evenly over the fish. Bake until the fish flakes easily with a fork.

SERVES 3 TO 4

Bourbon-Glazed Salmon

1 cup packed brown sugar
6 tablespoons bourbon
1/4 cup soy sauce
2 tablespoons lime juice
2 garlic cloves, minced
2 teaspoons grated fresh ginger

1/2 teaspoon salt
1/4 teaspoon pepper
1 1/2 pounds salmon fillets
4 teaspoons sesame seeds
1/2 cup chopped green onions

Combine the brown sugar, bourbon, soy sauce, lime juice, garlic, ginger, salt and pepper in a sealable plastic bag, mixing well. Add the salmon. Seal the bag and turn to coat evenly. Marinate in the refrigerator for 30 minutes, turning the bag after 15 minutes.

Preheat a grill or broiler. Drain the salmon, discarding the marinade. Grill or broil the salmon for 8 to 11 minutes or until it flakes easily. Place on a serving plate and sprinkle with the sesame seeds and green onions.

SERVES 2

125

Chinook Salmon

Salmon symbolizes the Pacific Northwest's culinary heritage and native American lore. Many tribes believed that salmon sacrificed themselves to benefit humankind. When a Chinook fisherman caught the season's first salmon, the fish was eaten ceremonially. Today there are still many salmon celebrations throughout the region to honor the first salmon of the season. Chinook, or King Salmon, is the largest of the species, averaging twenty-five pounds and growing as large as one hundred pounds. Young Chinook spend three months to two years in fresh water before starting their journey to the ocean. They remain at sea for one to six years before returning to their freshwater rivers and streams of origin. They spawn once and then die.

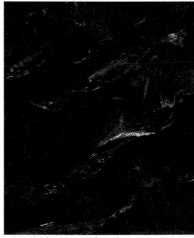

Reprinted with permission of
The Olympian/Steven Herppich

Blackened Salmon

1 tablespoon paprika
2 teaspoons salt
1 teaspoon freshly ground
    black pepper
1 teaspoon cayenne pepper
1 teaspoon onion powder

1 teaspoon garlic powder
$1/2$ teaspoon dried oregano
$1/2$ teaspoon dried thyme
2 pounds boneless salmon fillets
$1/2$ cup (1 stick) unsalted
    butter, melted

Preheat a grill. Mix the paprika, salt, black pepper, cayenne pepper, onion powder, garlic powder, oregano and thyme together in a shallow dish. Dip the salmon in the butter and coat both sides with the seasoning mixture, pressing lightly. Grill the fish until done to taste.

SERVES 6

Salmon with Blackberry Hollandaise

3 cups fish stock
2 cups white wine
1 lemon, cut into quarters
1 sprig of fresh mint
4 (6-ounce) salmon fillets

Blackberry Hollandaise
    (page 127)
Reserved blackberry purée
    (page 127)

Combine the stock, wine, lemon and mint in a saucepan. Bring to a boil and then reduce the heat to a simmer. Place the salmon fillets carefully in the saucepan using a spatula. Poach for 8 to 10 minutes or just until cooked through.

Spoon a small amount of Blackberry Hollandaise in the center of each of four serving plates; drizzle a thin circle of the reserved blackberry purée in the Blackberry Hollandaise. Draw the back of a spoon through the sauce from the center toward the edge of the plates, making a scalloped effect.

Place the salmon fillets in the sauce on the plates, taking care that they retain their shape. Garnish each plate with mint or borage flowers and three to five fresh blackberries.

SERVES 4

Blackberry Hollandaise

4 egg yolks
2 tablespoons fresh lemon juice
3/4 cup (1 1/2 sticks) unsalted
   butter, melted
Dash of salt
Dash of white pepper

2 cups blackberries
3 tablespoons madeira
1 teaspoon Dijon mustard
1/2 teaspoon minced garlic
1/2 teaspoon minced shallot
Juice of 1 lemon

Whisk the egg yolks and 2 tablespoons lemon juice together in a double boiler. Place the pan over simmering water, allowing space between the water and the pan. Cook just until the mixture begins to thicken, whisking constantly. Remove from the heat and add the butter in a steady stream, whisking constantly to incorporate completely. Season with salt and white pepper.

Combine the blackberries with the wine, Dijon mustard, garlic, shallot and juice of one lemon in a saucepan. Cook until reduced by one-fourth, stirring frequently to avoid scorching. Purée in a food processor and strain through a fine sieve into a bowl.

Reserve one-fourth of the blackberry purée for presentation. Fold the remaining purée into the hollandaise sauce.

MAKES ABOUT 3 CUPS

127

Caramelized Salmon in Soy Sauce and Grand Marnier

4 (6- to 8-ounce) salmon fillets
  with skin
2 tablespoons grated
  fresh ginger
1/2 cup cilantro, chopped

1 tablespoon vegetable oil
1 cup sugar
1/2 cup soy sauce
1/2 cup Grand Marnier

Sprinkle the cut side of the salmon fillets with the ginger and cilantro. Marinate, covered, in the refrigerator for 3 to 24 hours.

Heat the oil in a large skillet or sauté pan over medium-high heat. Coat the cut sides of the salmon with the sugar and place sugar side down in the skillet. Sear for 2 to 3 minutes until the sugar begins to caramelize. Flip the salmon fillets skin side down.

Remove the skillet from the heat and add the soy sauce and Grand Marnier. Return to the heat and cook until the salmon is cooked to medium or to taste.

SERVES 4

Chef Jeff Busch

This salmon recipe is full of flavor with just a few simple ingredients. Jeff Busch, chef and owner of Bella Sera Catering in Spokane, Washington, suggests substituting water and a tablespoon of grated orange zest if you prefer not to cook with alcohol. This will infuse the salmon with the same citrus flavor.

Hoisin-Baked Salmon

2 tablespoons hoisin sauce
2 teaspoons soy sauce
Few drops of sesame oil
1/4 teaspoon chili paste

2 (6-ounce) salmon fillets
1 to 2 teaspoons white or black
 sesame seeds

Preheat the oven to 375 degrees. Combine the hoisin sauce, soy sauce and sesame oil in a bowl. Stir in the chile paste. Brush or spoon the mixture over the salmon in a baking dish. Sprinkle with the sesame seeds. Bake for 8 to 10 minutes or until the salmon flakes easily with a fork.

SERVES 2

Rainbow Trout with Chanterelle Mushrooms

4 rainbow trout, heads removed
Lemon pepper to taste
Fresh or dried tarragon to taste
2 lemons, sliced

1 pound fresh chanterelle
 mushrooms
1 tablespoon butter

Preheat the oven to 350 degrees. Place the trout in a foil-lined 9×13-inch baking dish. Sprinkle lemon pepper and tarragon in the cavity of each trout and line with the lemon slices.

Sauté the mushrooms in the butter in a skillet. Spoon over the trout. Cover the dish with foil and bake for 45 minutes.

SERVES 4

Capturing the Wild Mushroom

The Pacific Northwest is ideal for mushroom gatherers. The mild, damp climate and rich forest soils are home to delectable wild mushrooms, including oyster, boletus, morel, matsutake, and the local favorite, chanterelles. Chanterelles, native to the region, are the treasures of the woods. Their mild apricot scent and delicate earthy flavor make them highly desirable with cooks in the Northwest.

Clam and Vegetable Linguini

2 tablespoons extra-virgin
  olive oil
1/2 onion, chopped
3 garlic cloves, crushed
2 cups sliced mushrooms
1 red bell pepper, chopped
1 zucchini, thickly sliced
1 (10-ounce) can baby clams
1 (16-ounce) can chopped
  tomatoes

1 teaspoon basil
1 teaspoon parsley
1/2 teaspoon oregano
1/2 teaspoon thyme
1 teaspoon salt
1/2 teaspoon cracked pepper
16 ounces linguini, cooked
  and drained
1 cup (4 ounces) shredded
  Parmesan cheese

Heat the olive oil in a large skillet and add the onion. Sauté just until the onion begins to brown. Add the garlic and sauté until heated through. Add the mushrooms, bell pepper and zucchini and sauté for 2 minutes.

Drain the clams, reserving half the liquid. Add the clams and reserved clam liquid, the tomatoes, basil, parsley, oregano, thyme, salt and pepper. Simmer, covered, for 5 minutes.

Combine with the linguini in a bowl and toss to mix well. Top with the cheese and serve warm.

SERVES 6

South Sound Steamer Clams

1 1/2 to 2 pounds Manila clams, butter clams
    or littleneck clams
1/4 cup chopped tomato
1 garlic clove, minced
2 tablespoons minced green onions
1/4 cup (1/2 stick) butter, melted (optional)

Place the clams in a large stockpot and cover; do not add water, as the clams will release enough nectar as they heat. Place over high heat and cook until steam begins to rise. Add the tomato, garlic and green onions.

Steam, covered, for 2 minutes per pound or until the clams on the top have opened up; discard any clams that fail to open.

Place the clams in individual bowls or mound on a platter. Add some of the nectar to each bowl or serve it in a bowl on the side. Serve with the butter if desired, but you may find the clams are so sweet that you will not want it. Serve with French bread or garlic bread to soak up the flavorful nectar.

SERVES 2 AS AN ENTRÉE OR
3 TO 4 AS AN APPETIZER

131

Clam Juice

It may seem strange to "steam" clams without adding any liquid, but you will find that the nectar released by the clams during cooking is more than enough liquid to steam them. True clam lovers will pour the nectar into a mug and enjoy it with their clams, either sipped or sopped up with warm crusty bread.

Curried Oysters

1 pint small or extra-small fresh
   oysters packed in their
   own liquor
1 1/2 cups (about) milk
3 tablespoons all-purpose flour
1 teaspoon yellow curry
1 teaspoon sugar
1/2 teaspoon salt
3 tablespoons butter

2 tablespoons minced onion
2 teaspoons grated fresh ginger
Hot cooked rice
Condiments such as Mango
   Chutney (below), crumbled
   crisp-cooked bacon, flaked
   coconut, and/or
   chopped peanuts

Pour the oysters with their liquor into a medium saucepan and cook over medium heat just until the edges begin to curl. Remove the oysters to a bowl with a slotted spoon; tent with foil to keep warm. Pour the liquor into a 2-cup measuring cup and add enough of the milk to measure 2 cups. Mix the flour with the curry, sugar and salt in a small bowl.

Melt the butter in the same saucepan. Add the onion and ginger and sauté for 3 minutes. Stir in the flour mixture and cook for 1 minute, stirring constantly. Add the milk mixture and cook over medium heat until thickened, stirring constantly.

Add the oysters to the sauce with a slotted spoon and cook for 1 to 2 minutes or until heated through. Remove from the heat and serve over rice with the condiments of choice.

SERVES 3 OR 4

Mango Chutney

Mango Chutney goes well with Curried Oysters. Cut 1 mango into 1/2-inch pieces and combine with 1 minced small red onion, 1 tablespoon minced fresh mint, 2 tablespoons honey and 1 minced small jalapeño chile in a bowl. Season with salt and pepper and let stand for one hour to develop the flavors.

Ginger-Lime Shrimp with Sweet Potato Mash

1/4 cup finely chopped red onion
1 tablespoon olive oil
1/2 cup finely chopped mango
2 garlic cloves, minced
2 teaspoons minced fresh ginger

11/2 pounds peeled deveined shrimp
1/4 cup fresh lime juice
1/4 cup minced fresh cilantro
Dash of cayenne pepper
Sweet Potato Mash (below)

Heat a large skillet over medium-high heat. Sauté the onion in the olive oil in the skillet for 3 minutes. Add the mango, garlic and ginger and sauté for 1 minute or until fragrant and sizzling. Add the shrimp and cook for 2 to 3 minutes or until cooked through, stirring frequently. Remove the shrimp to a warm plate using a slotted spoon and cover with foil.

Increase the heat to high and heat the skillet for 1 minute. Add the lime juice, cilantro and cayenne pepper to the skillet. Cook for 2 minutes or until slightly reduced, stirring constantly.

Spoon Sweet Potato Mash onto four plates or into four bowls. Arrange the shrimp over the sweet potatoes and spoon the sauce over the top. Serve immediately.

SERVES 4

Sweet Potato Mash

3 large sweet potatoes or yams
2 tablespoons butter
2 teaspoons minced fresh ginger

11/2 teaspoons kosher salt
1/4 cup half-and-half

Preheat the oven to 375 degrees. Place the sweet potatoes on a baking sheet and bake for 45 minutes or until tender. Let cool slightly, cut into halves and peel.

Combine the sweet potatoes with the butter, ginger and kosher salt in a food processor or mixing bowl. Process or beat with a hand mixer or potato masher until smooth. Add the half-and-half and mix well. Tent with foil to keep warm until serving time.

SERVES 4

Lemon Shrimp Linguini

2 tablespoons extra-virgin
   olive oil
3 garlic cloves, minced
2 cups sliced mushrooms
1 pound shrimp, peeled
   and deveined
1/2 cup chicken broth
2 pounds fresh spinach
1 teaspoon dried basil
1/2 teaspoon dried oregano

1/2 teaspoon cracked pepper
16 ounces linguini
1 cup (2 sticks) butter, melted
2 tablespoons lemon juice
Salt to taste
3 tablespoons toasted pine nuts
2 tablespoons minced
   fresh parsley
1/2 cup (2 ounces) shredded
   Parmesan cheese

Heat the olive oil in a large skillet over medium heat and add the garlic. Sauté until the garlic is heated through. Add the mushrooms and sauté for 2 minutes. Add the shrimp and sauté just until they begin to turn pink. Stir in the broth, spinach, basil, oregano and pepper. Simmer for 5 minutes.

Cook the pasta using the package directions; drain. Combine with the butter, lemon juice and salt in a bowl and toss to mix well. Spoon onto four serving plates and top with the shrimp mixture. Sprinkle with pine nuts, parsley and cheese.

SERVES 4

134

Inspiration

We all celebrate birthdays and anniversaries to commemorate significant milestones in our lives, and the Junior League of Olympia (JLO) is no different. When JLO reached fifteen years of service, we celebrated by collaborating with city officials to build the **Decatur Woods Playground** in a transitional neighborhood. JLO is committed to improving the quality of life for children in our community.

Shrimp with Feta Cheese

8 ounces mushrooms, sliced
1 tablespoon olive oil
1 tablespoon butter
Salt and black pepper to taste
2 pounds shrimp, peeled and
   deveined
2 tablespoons olive oil
1 large onion, chopped
2 garlic cloves, minced

1 (12-ounce) can crushed
   Italian tomatoes
1/3 cup dry white wine
1/4 teaspoon ground cumin
1/4 teaspoon crushed red
   pepper flakes, or to taste
4 ounces feta cheese, crumbled
4 cups cooked white rice
1/2 cup chopped fresh parsley

Sauté the mushrooms in 1 tablespoon olive oil and the butter in a saucepan. Season with salt and black pepper. Combine with the shrimp in a 9×13-inch baking pan.

Heat 2 tablespoons olive oil in a skillet and add the onion. Sauté over medium heat until translucent. Add the garlic, tomatoes, wine, cumin and red pepper flakes. Cook for 25 minutes or until thickened.

Preheat the oven to 450 degrees. Spoon the sauce over the shrimp mixture in the baking pan and top with the cheese. Bake for 15 to 20 minutes or until the shrimp are pink and cooked through. Serve over the rice and sprinkle with the fresh parsley.

SERVES 6

Sides

SIDES

◀ CRANBERRY-STUFFED WINTER SQUASH

Sesame-Glazed Bok Choy

1 tablespoon sesame seeds
1 1/2 tablespoons rice vinegar
1 1/2 tablespoons soy sauce
2 teaspoons toasted sesame oil
1/2 teaspoon sugar

1 to 3 bunches bok choy
3 tablespoons peanut oil
1 handful minced garlic flowers
1 tablespoon minced
   fresh ginger

Toast the sesame seeds in a skillet for 2 to 3 minutes or until golden brown. Combine the rice vinegar, soy sauce, sesame oil and sugar in a bowl and mix well.

Cut larger bok choy bunches into quarters or smaller bunches into halves lengthwise. Heat 1 1/2 tablesepoons of the peanut oil in a large skillet over high heat. Add the bok choy cut side down and sauté for 2 minutes or until light brown. Turn the bok choy over and sauté for 1 minute longer. Remove to a platter.

Heat the remaining 1 1/2 tablesepoons peanut oil in the skillet and then add the garlic flowers and ginger. Stir-fry until golden brown. Add the rice vinegar mixture and simmer for 30 seconds. Return the bok choy to the skillet and cook for 30 seconds longer. Sprinkle with the sesame seeds and serve immediately.

SERVES 4

Stir-Fried Bok Choy with Cilantro and Toasted Peanuts

3 to 4 tablespoons whole
   raw peanuts
1 teaspoon peanut oil
1/8 teaspoon red pepper flakes
Salt to taste
1 bunch bok choy
1 teaspoon peanut oil

1 onion, finely chopped
4 teaspoons minced fresh ginger
1 teaspoon cornstarch
3 tablespoons cold water
2 tablespoons soy sauce
1 bunch cilantro, chopped

Sauté the peanuts in 1 teaspoon peanut oil in a skillet until golden brown. Chop the peanuts and combine with the red pepper flakes and salt in a small bowl.

Slice off the stems of the bok choy, leaving the leaves whole; cut the stems into 1/2-inch pieces. Heat 1 teaspoon peanut oil in a wok or heavy saucepan over high heat. Add the onion and ginger and stir-fry for 1 minute. Add the bok choy and stir-fry until wilted and glossy.

Blend the cornstarch with the water and soy sauce in a cup. Add the cornstarch mixture and cilantro to the bok choy. Stir-fry for 1 to 2 minutes. Add the peanut mixture and serve warm.

SERVES 4

Broccoli with Browned Butter and Mizithra Cheese

Florets of 1 large head broccoli
1/4 cup (1/2 stick) butter
2 ounces finely grated aged mizithra cheese,
    crumbled feta cheese or grated Romano cheese

Steam the broccoli with a small amount of water in a saucepan for 4 minutes or until tender. Drain in a colander and place in a serving bowl.

Melt the butter in a small saucepan over medium-high heat. Cook until the butter is light to medium brown, swirling the saucepan occasionally. Remove from the heat and continue to swirl the saucepan several times. Pour over the broccoli and toss to coat well. Sprinkle with the cheese and serve immediately.

SERVES 6

It's Greek to Me

Mizithra is a Greek cheese with a strong, salty flavor. Browned butter with mizithra is usually paired with pasta, but this preparation makes everyday broccoli a delicious accompaniment to any meal! The browned butter provides a nutty flavor. The darker the butter, the stronger the flavor, but it can also burn, so watch it carefully.

Roasted Carrots

1 or 2 bunches carrots
2 tablespoons olive oil

1/2 teaspoon salt

Preheat the oven to 475 degrees. Toss the carrots with the olive oil and salt in a large baking pan. Spread into a single layer and place on the center oven rack. Roast for 12 minutes; shake the pan and toss the carrots. Roast for 8 to 10 minutes longer or until brown and tender.

SERVES 4 TO 6

Roasted Carrots in Maple Browned Butter

1 or 2 bunches carrots
1 1/2 teaspoons olive oil
1/2 teaspoon salt

1 tablespoon butter
1 tablespoon maple syrup

Preheat the oven to 475 degrees. Prepare the carrots with the olive oil and salt as in the recipe above. Melt the butter in a saucepan over medium heat and cook until deep golden brown, stirring occasionally. Remove from the heat and stir in the maple syrup. Drizzle over the carrots. Roast for 8 to 10 minutes longer or until brown and tender.

SERVES 4 TO 6

141

Roasted Carrots with Ginger-Orange Glaze

1 or 2 bunches carrots
2 tablespoons olive oil
1/2 teaspoon salt

1 tablespoon water
1 tablespoon orange marmalade
1/2 teaspoon grated fresh ginger

Preheat the oven to 475 degrees. Prepare the carrots with the olive oil and salt as in the recipe above. Bring the water, marmalade and ginger to a boil in a saucepan. Drizzle over the carrots and roast for 8 to 10 minutes longer or until brown and tender.

SERVES 4 TO 6

Roasted Cauliflower with Cherry Tomatoes and Olives

Florets of 1 large
   head cauliflower
1 pint cherry tomatoes
3/4 cup pitted kalamata olives
3 tablespoons olive oil

1/2 teaspoon salt
Pinch of red pepper flakes
2 tablespoons chopped
   fresh basil

Preheat the oven to 425 degrees. Combine the cauliflower, tomatoes and olives in a large bowl. Drizzle with the olive oil and mix to coat well. Sprinkle with the salt and pepper flakes; mix well.

Spread on a baking sheet with a rim. Roast for 20 minutes or until the cauliflower is tender and the edges are golden brown. Sprinkle with the basil and serve immediately.

SERVES 6 TO 8

Chef Kathy Casey

When cauliflower is oven-roasted, its sweetness is intensified, giving it a delectable new character. Chef Kathy Casey is a food, beverage, and restaurant consultant and food writer. She owns Kathy Casey Food Studios® and co-owns John Casey Dish D'Lish® with her husband, with locations in Seattle and at Sea-Tac International Airport. Her most recent book is the James Beard Award-nominated *Kathy Casey's Northwest Table*. For relaxation, she loves to fish and hunt wild mushrooms.

Swiss Chard with Raisins and Pine Nuts

1/2 cup pine nuts
Salt to taste
1 bunch Swiss chard
1 onion, finely chopped

1 tablespoon olive oil
1/4 cup golden raisins
1 cup water
Pepper to taste

Toast the pine nuts in a wide heavy 6- to 8-quart saucepan over medium heat for 1 to 1 1/2 minutes or until golden brown, stirring constantly. Remove with a slotted spoon and drain on paper towels; season with salt.

Separate the chard leaves from the stems and coarsely chop both, keeping the leaves and stems separate.

Sauté the onion in the olive oil in the saucepan for 1 minute, stirring occasionally. Add the chard stems and sauté for 2 minutes. Add the raisins and 1/2 cup of the water. Reduce the heat and simmer for 3 minutes or until the stems are tender.

Add the chard leaves and the remaining 1/2 cup water. Simmer, partially covered, for 3 minutes or until tender, stirring occasionally. Season with salt and pepper. Spoon into a serving bowl and sprinkle with the pine nuts.

SERVES 4

143

Tolmie State Park

The magnificent outdoors is a way of life in the Pacific Northwest. Tolmie State Park is an ideal destination for the outdoor enthusiast. Located on Nisqually Beach, Tolmie State Park is a 105-acre marine park that stretches 1,800 feet along the stunning Puget Sound saltwater shoreline. Park visitors enjoy searching for marine life in the tide pools and saltwater marshes; hiking on the lush, vibrant forested trails; scuba diving in the underwater park; kayaking in the Sound; or simply taking a stroll on the beach. Wildlife and marine birds are abundant, and majestic bald eagles often soar through the park.

Reprinted with permission of
The Olympian/Tony Overman

Baked Walla Walla Onions

4 Walla Walla onions or other sweet onions
2 beef bouillon cubes or vegetable bouillon cubes,
    cut into halves
4 teaspoons butter
4 teaspoons brown sugar

Preheat the oven to 350 degrees. Cut a slice from the top and bottom of each onion so they sit flat. Place root end up and scoop out a hole just big enough to hold half a bouillon cube. Place the bouillon cube halves in the holes and top evenly with the butter and brown sugar.

Wrap each onion in heavy-duty foil, pulling up the sides to enclose the onion completely and sealing the top securely. Place in a baking dish. Bake for 1 hour. Open the foil carefully to avoid escaping steam and place the onions and cooking liquid in soup bowls to serve.

This can also be prepared on a grill. Wrap the onions in a double layer of heavy-duty foil and place directly on the grill. Grill, with the lid closed, for 1 hour.

SERVES 4

How Sweet It Is

Walla Walla onions are renowned throughout the United States for their mild, crisp, sweet flavor. These summertime sweet onions only grow in the Walla Walla Valley of Washington and a small section of northeastern Oregon. They were brought to the Northwest from Italy more than a century ago. The sweetness from these highly sought-after onions comes from a low sulfur content in the soil. Walla Walla onions caramelize like a dream, are delicious uncooked, and complement a variety of ingredients.

Cougar Gold Mashed Potatoes

3 quarts water
1 pound Yukon Gold potatoes
    or red potatoes, peeled
    or unpeeled
3 garlic cloves, minced
1/4 cup (1/2 stick) butter

1 cup heavy cream
Salt and pepper to taste
1 cup (4 ounces) shredded
    Cougar Gold cheese or other
    sharp Cheddar cheese

Bring the water to a boil in a large saucepan and add the potatoes. Cook until the potatoes are tender; drain.

Sauté the garlic in a small amount of the butter in a medium saucepan. Add the remaining butter, the cream, salt and pepper to the garlic. Heat until the butter melts and the cream is warm. Whisk in the cheese gradually. Add the cream mixture to the potatoes and beat or whip until smooth. Garnish with chopped chives or green onions.

For Twice-Baked Potatoes, bake the potatoes, cut into halves and scoop the cooked potato pulp from the skins. Prepare as above and stuff the mashed potatoes into the reserved skins. Top with additional cheese and chives and broil until golden brown.

For Won Ton Potatoes, fit won ton wrappers into muffin cups sprayed with nonstick cooking spray. Bake at 400 degrees for 8 to 10 minutes or until light brown. Spoon the mashed potatoes into the shells and sprinkle with chives or green onions.

SERVES 4

As Good as Cougar Gold

The Palouse Valley is nestled in the southeast corner of Washington State. It is known for its wheat fields, the Washington State University Cougars, and it is also the home of a delicious cheese with a nutty flavor: Cougar Gold cheese. The sharp white Cheddar cheese somewhat resembles Swiss cheese or Gouda cheese, and because of its popularity is sold exclusively in thirty-ounce tin cans.

Cranberry-Stuffed Winter Squash

2 small winter squash, such as acorn, delicata or sweet dumpling
1 tablespoon unsalted butter, melted
Salt to taste
3 tablespoons unsalted butter
1/2 cup minced shallots or finely chopped yellow onion
1 teaspoon minced garlic
2 cups coarsely chopped tart apples
1/2 cup chopped cranberries
1/2 teaspoon cinnamon
1/4 teaspoon grated fresh nutmeg
1 cup fine dry plain bread crumbs
1 cup (4 ounces) shredded Cheddar cheese, pepper Jack cheese or Swiss cheese
4 ounces sliced smoked bacon, crisp-cooked and crumbled
1/2 cup pecans, chopped

Preheat the oven to 400 degrees. Cut the squash into halves lengthwise, discarding the seeds and membranes. Brush the cut sides with 1 tablespoon butter and season with salt. Arrange cut side down in a lightly greased baking pan. Add 1/2 inch hot water. Bake for 35 to 45 minutes or just until barely tender when tested with a wooden pick.

Melt 3 tablespoons butter in a skillet over medium-high heat. Add the shallots and sauté for 4 minutes or until tender-crisp. Add the garlic, apples and cranberries. Sauté for 4 minutes or until the apples are tender. Stir in the cinnamon and nutmeg.

Combine the bread crumbs, cheese and apple mixture in a bowl and mix well. Turn the squash cut side up in the baking dish and mound the stuffing lightly into the centers. Spoon any remaining stuffing around the squash to hold them erect. Bake for 20 minutes or until the cheese melts. Sprinkle with the bacon and pecans. Serve hot.

SERVES 4

Crazy Cranberries

Fresh cranberries can be found in abundance as fall arrives in the Pacific Northwest. In addition to the good, old-fashioned cranberry sauce that is associated with holiday meals, these bright red berries can add a distinctive flavor to vegetables, salads, and breads.

Squash with Cashews

1 delicata squash
3 tablespoons rice vinegar
3 tablespoons soy sauce
1 tablespoon sesame oil
1 teaspoon sugar

1 teaspoon minced garlic
1 teaspoon minced fresh ginger
1 teaspoon peanut oil
1/2 cup unsalted cashews,
    roasted and chopped

Preheat the oven to 350 degrees. Cut the squash into halves, discarding the seeds and membranes. Place cut side down in a small amount of water in a microwave-safe dish. Microwave on High for 5 to 6 minutes or until partially cooked. Let stand until cool enough to handle.

Cut into 1-inch pieces; the squash should measure about 3 cups. Place in a 11/2- to 2-quart baking dish and bake for 20 to 25 minutes or until tender. Mix the rice vinegar, soy sauce, sesame oil and sugar in a bowl. Sauté the garlic and ginger in the peanut oil in a skillet over medium heat for 1 to 2 minutes. Add the rice vinegar mixture and cook until heated through. Pour over the squash and mix lightly, taking care not to mash the squash. Top with the cashews and cover to keep warm.

SERVES 4

Fiesta Squash

3 cups (1/2-inch slices) yellow
    summer squash
1 onion, chopped
1 (8-ounce) can chopped
    green chiles
3/4 cup mayonnaise
2 eggs, beaten

4 ounces sharp Cheddar
    cheese, shredded
1/2 teaspoon freshly ground
    pepper, or to taste
11/2 to 2 cups bread crumbs,
    or 1 sleeve butter
    crackers, crushed

Preheat the oven to 350 degrees. Combine the squash with a small amount of water in a microwave-safe dish. Microwave on High for 3 minutes or until tender-crisp; drain. Mix with the onion, green chiles, mayonnaise, eggs, cheese and pepper in a large bowl. Spoon into a lightly greased 2-quart baking dish. Top with the bread crumbs. Bake for 30 to 40 minutes or until bubbly.

SERVES 6

Tomatoes Stuffed with Spinach

1 or 2 (10-ounce) packages
    frozen spinach
8 ounces cream cheese, softened
Salt and pepper to taste
3/4 cup canned or frozen
    artichoke hearts, chopped

1/2 cup chopped green onions
1 tablespoon butter
6 tomatoes
1/4 cup bread crumbs
1/4 cup (1 ounce) grated
    Parmesan cheese

Preheat the oven to 350 degrees. Cook the spinach using the package directions; drain. Combine with the cream cheese in a bowl; season with salt and pepper. Stir to melt the cream cheese. Sauté the artichoke hearts and green onions in the butter in a skillet. Add to the spinach mixture and mix well.

Cut off the tops of the tomatoes and scoop out the seeds and membranes. Spoon the spinach mixture into the tomato shells. Sprinkle with the bread crumbs and Parmesan cheese. Arrange in a baking dish. Bake until the spinach is heated through and the topping is golden brown.

SERVES 6

Mashed Chipotle Yams

1 1/2 pounds yams
    (about 3 large yams)
1 chipotle chile packed in
    adobo sauce

3 tablespoons butter, melted
2 teaspoons adobo sauce, or
    to taste

Preheat the oven to 425 degrees. Pierce the skins of the yams and place in a glass baking dish. Bake for 40 to 50 minutes or until fork-tender. Cool slightly. Process the chile and butter in a blender or food processor until puréed. Cut the yams into halves and scoop the pulp from the shells into a bowl. Add the chile mixture and mash with a potato masher until smooth. Add the adobo sauce. Serve with grilled beef, pork or chicken.

SERVES 6

Vegetable Stacks

4 (1/2-inch) slices eggplant
4 (1/2-inch) slices squash
    (zucchini, patty pan
    or crookneck)
2 eggs, beaten
1/2 cup bread crumbs

4 mushrooms, sliced
4 slices mozzarella cheese or
    other flavorful cheese
4 slices tomato
Chopped fresh or dried basil
    to taste

Preheat the oven to 400 degrees. Dip the eggplant and squash slices in the eggs and then coat with the bread crumbs. Arrange on a baking sheet and bake for 10 minutes.

Place the mushrooms in a microwave-safe dish. Microwave on High for 1 minute. Layer the eggplant, cheese, squash and tomato in four stacks in a baking dish. Sprinkle the stacks with basil and top with the mushrooms. Bake until the cheese melts.

SERVES 4

149

Inspirational

Every child needs a safe and reliable place to go after school. The Junior League of Olympia (JLO) recognizes the importance of after-school programs and reaches out in the community to support those organizations that support our kids. **The Evergreen Vista Homework Club** has benefited from hundreds of JLO volunteer hours, which provided a facelift for the facility, and continued support with supplies, food, and room decorations. The atmosphere is one that the kids are proud to be a part of and inspires them to learn.

Asparagus Couscous

12 fresh asparagus spears, or
   2/3 cup fresh or frozen peas
1 cup fresh orange juice
1/2 cup water
1 tablespoon olive oil
1 garlic clove, minced
1/4 cup dried currants

1/2 cup smoked almonds,
   chopped
1/4 teaspoon salt
1/8 teaspoon freshly
   ground pepper
11/2 cups Moroccan couscous

Snap off the tough woody ends of the asparagus spears and cut the spears into 1-inch pieces. Combine with the juice, water, olive oil, garlic, currants, almonds, salt and pepper in a saucepan. Bring to a boil and cook for 3 minutes. Remove from the heat and stir in the couscous. Let stand, covered, for 5 minutes. Fluff with a fork and serve warm or at room temperature with grilled seafood or meat.

SERVES 4 TO 6

Quick Pasta

Couscous is actually coarsely ground semolina pasta. Moroccan couscous is the smallest variety and cooks very quickly, usually in less than five minutes. Israeli and Lebanese couscous grains are larger and are typically cooked longer, either steamed or stirred like risotto. Couscous will absorb the flavors of the cooking liquid and seasonings while cooking.

Polenta with Asparagus and Balsamic Butter

1 pound fresh asparagus, trimmed
1 teaspoon olive oil
1/4 teaspoon minced garlic
Pinch of salt
1 1/2 cups milk or half-and-half
1 1/2 cups water
1 cup polenta (corn grits)

1 cup (4 ounces) shredded Cheddar cheese and/or Monterey Jack cheese, or 1/2 to 3/4 cup (2 to 3 ounces) grated Gruyère cheese
2 tablespoons butter
2 teaspoons soy sauce
1 teaspoon balsamic vinegar

Stir-fry the asparagus in the heated olive oil in a skillet for 3 minutes. Add the garlic and salt and stir-fry for 3 minutes longer.

Bring the milk and water to a boil in a saucepan. Stir in the polenta and cook until thickened, stirring carefully to avoid splatters. Stir in the cheese until melted. Cook for 5 minutes longer. Remove from the heat.

Brown the butter lightly in a skillet. Remove from the heat and stir in the soy sauce and balsamic vinegar. Spoon the polenta onto serving plates and top with the asparagus. Drizzle with the balsamic butter.

To prepare in ramekins, line ramekins with strips of baking parchment, allowing the ends to overhang the sides. Cut the asparagus to lengths the height of the ramekins. Line the sides of the ramekins with the asparagus, reserving the tips for garnish. Reduce the cooking time for the polenta by 5 minutes. Spoon it into the ramekins. Bake at 350 degrees for 15 to 20 minutes or until light brown. Let stand for 5 minutes and invert onto serving plates. Top with the reserved asparagus tips and drizzle with the balsamic butter.

SERVES 6 TO 8

151

Spring's Abundance: Asparagus

Washington's spring weather brings warm days and cool nights—perfect conditions for tender and sweet asparagus, which will sometimes grow seven to nine inches in one day. The simplest way to prepare asparagus is to grill or sauté it over high heat to caramelize the sugars and intensify the flavor.

Reprinted with permission of
The Olympian/Steven Herppich

Butternut Squash and Leek Risotto

1 (2-pound) butternut squash
2 tablespoons (about) olive oil
6 to 8 cups chicken stock or canned low-salt chicken broth
2 tablespoons olive oil
3 large leeks, white and pale green portions only, thinly sliced (about 3 cups)
2 cups arborio rice or other medium-grain rice

1/2 cup dry white wine
1/2 cup whipping cream or fat-free half-and-half
1/2 cup (2 ounces) grated Parmesan cheese
2 tablespoons chopped fresh sage
Salt and pepper to taste

Preheat the oven to 450 degrees. Cut the squash lengthwise into halves and discard the seeds. Brush the cut sides with about 2 tablespoons olive oil. Place cut side down on a baking sheet coated with additional olive oil. Roast for 25 to 30 minutes or until tender. Cool, peel and cut into 1/2-inch pieces.

Bring the stock to a boil in a large heavy saucepan. Reduce the heat to very low; cover and maintain at a simmer.

Heat 2 tablespoons olive oil in a large heavy saucepan over medium-low heat. Add the leeks and sauté for 10 minutes or until tender but not brown. Add the rice and sauté for 1 minute. Add the wine and simmer for 2 minutes or until it is absorbed, stirring constantly.

Add the heated stock 1/2 cup at a time, cooking until the stock is absorbed after each addition and stirring frequently for about 25 minutes or until the rice is tender and creamy; use as much stock as needed.

Add the roasted squash, cream, cheese and sage. Cook until heated through. Season with salt and pepper and serve warm.

SERVES 4 AS A MAIN COURSE OR 6 AS A FIRST COURSE

White Wine Risotto with Porcini and Rapini

2 ounces dried porcini
  mushrooms
2 (14-ounce) cans chicken stock
  or vegetable stock
1/4 cup minced onion
8 ounces rapini (Chinese
  broccoli or broccoli
  rabe), chopped
1 tablespoon olive oil
1 teaspoon lemon juice
1 1/2 cups arborio rice
1 tablespoon olive oil
1/2 cup white wine
2 tablespoons butter, softened
2 tablespoons grated
  Parmigiano-Reggiano cheese
1 teaspoon fresh thyme
Salt and pepper to taste

Soak the mushrooms in hot water in a bowl for 5 minutes or longer. Drain, reserving the liquid. Add enough of the reserved liquid to the stock to measure 4 cups. Bring the stock mixture to a boil in a saucepan. Reduce the heat and maintain at a simmer.

Sauté the mushrooms, onion, rapini and garlic in 1 tablespoon olive oil in a heated sauté pan until the onion is translucent. Stir in the lemon juice.

Sauté the rice in 1 tablespoon olive oil in a heavy saucepan for 2 minutes. Add the wine and stir to deglaze the saucepan.

Add the stock 1/2 cup at a time, cooking until the liquid is absorbed after each addition and stirring constantly for 20 minutes or until the rice is cooked al dente. Add the sautéed vegetables, butter, cheese and thyme. Season with salt and pepper.

SERVES 6

Risotto 101

Arborio rice is used in risotto because it absorbs liquids without breaking down. Sauté the aromatics (such as onions, shallots, or garlic) and the rice in butter until the rice is translucent. Add the hot liquids (such as stock, wine, or water) one-half cup at a time, stirring constantly. Adding more liquid only when the previous addition has been absorbed gives risotto its creamy texture. Add the cheeses, dairy products, and vegetables at the last minute.

Dilled Green Beans

4 pounds whole fresh
    green beans
8 dried hot red chiles
4 teaspoons whole
    mustard seeds
4 teaspoons dill seeds

8 garlic cloves
5 cups cider vinegar
5 cups water
6 tablespoons canning salt or
    pickling salt

Pack the beans into eight (1-pint) jars. Add 1 hot chile, $1/2$ teaspoon mustard seeds, $1/2$ teaspoon dill seeds and 1 garlic clove to each jar.

Combine the cider vinegar, water and canning salt in a saucepan and bring to a boil. Ladle into the jars, leaving $1/2$ inch headspace. Wipe the jar rims immediately and seal with 2-piece lids.

Place in a stockpot of boiling water and boil for 5 minutes. Cool to room temperature. Let stand for 4 weeks before serving.

YIELDS 8 (1-PINT) JARS

Spicy Carrot Pickles

1 (1-pound) bunch carrots,
    peeled and cut into $1/2$-inch
    pieces, or 1 pound
    baby carrots
6 to 8 whole garlic cloves
2 hot serranos or jalapeño chiles
    with seeds, sliced

1 onion, cut into $1/4$-inch rings
1 cup vinegar
1 cup water
$1/2$ teaspoon dried oregano
$1 1/2$ teaspoons salt

Combine the carrots with the garlic, serranos, and onion in a 1-quart jar. Combine the vinegar, water, oregano and salt in a small saucepan and bring to a boil. Pour over the carrot mixture in the jar. Cover tightly and chill in the refrigerator for 3 days or longer before serving.

Jalapeño chiles are milder than serranos. You can substitute zucchini or cauliflower for the carrots in this recipe.

YIELDS ONE (1-QUART) JAR

Chilled Red Pepper and Corn Relish

1 large red bell pepper
3 tablespoons pure maple syrup
1/4 cup cider vinegar
2 1/2 teaspoons hot red
  pepper sauce
2 teaspoons turmeric

1 teaspoon salt
1/3 cup vegetable oil
30 ounces fresh corn kernels
  or drained thawed
  frozen corn
1/2 cup sliced green onions

Roast the bell pepper under a broiler or over a gas flame until blackened on all sides. Place in a paper bag and let stand for 10 minutes. Peel and chop the bell pepper.

Combine the maple syrup, cider vinegar, hot sauce, turmeric and salt in a large bowl and mix well. Whisk in the oil gradually. Add the bell pepper, corn and green onions and toss to mix well. Marinate, covered, in the refrigerator for 8 to 24 hours. Let stand at room temperature for 30 minutes before serving. To store in the refrigerator for up to 3 days, omit the green onions until serving time.

SERVES 8

Beach House Barbecue Sauce

1 cup tomato purée
1 cup ketchup
2 tablespoons wine vinegar
2 tablespoons Worcestershire
  sauce
2 tablespoons mustard

1 1/2 tablespoons liquid smoke
2 tablespoons brown sugar
1 garlic clove, minced
1 tablespoon fennel seeds
3/4 teaspoon coarsely
  ground pepper

Combine the tomato purée, ketchup, wine vinegar, Worcestershire sauce, mustard and liquid smoke in a bowl and mix well. Stir in the brown sugar, garlic, fennel seeds and pepper. Serve with grilled chicken, pork or beef.

MAKES 2 1/2 CUPS

Desserts

DESSERTS

◀ PUMPKIN PISTACHIO PEAR CAKE

Hungarian Apple Pastry

4 or 5 baking apples, peeled
   and cored
3/4 cup sugar
2 teaspoons cinnamon

Processor Pastry (below)
1/4 cup sweet bread crumbs or
   wheat germ
1 small egg, beaten

Preheat the oven to 350 degrees. Grate the apples into a bowl and press to remove any excess moisture. Stir in the sugar and cinnamon.

Divide the Processor Pastry into two portions. Roll one portion into a 10×14-inch rectangle 1/4 inch thick. Spray the baking pan with nonstick baking spray and fit the pastry into the pan.

Layer half the bread crumbs, the apple mixture and the remaining bread crumbs in the prepared pan. Roll the remaining dough to fit the top and place over the apples; seal the edges. Brush with a mixture of the egg and a small amount of water.

Pierce the top pastry with a fork at 2-inch intervals. Bake for 30 minutes. Increase the oven temperature to 400 degrees and bake for 10 minutes longer. Cool on a wire rack and cut into 2-inch squares.

MAKES 35 SQUARES

158

Processor Pastry

3 cups all-purpose flour
1 cup confectioners' sugar
1/2 teaspoon baking powder
1 teaspoon salt

1 cup (2 sticks) margarine,
   chopped
1 egg
1/2 cup milk

Sift the flour, confectioners' sugar, baking powder and salt together. Combine with the margarine in a food processor; process until the mixture resembles coarse meal. Add the egg. Add the milk very gradually, processing constantly until the dough holds together. Shape into a ball and let stand in a cool place for 30 minutes.

MAKES TWO (10×14-INCH) PASTRIES

Apple Almond Dessert

2 to 3 cups sugar
2 to 3 cups water
5 or 6 Granny Smith apples, peeled, cored and thickly sliced

1 (8-ounce) can unsweetened almond paste
3 eggs

Preheat the oven to 350 degrees. Mix 2 cups of the sugar and 2 cups of the water in a large heavy saucepan. Cook until the sugar dissolves, stirring constantly. Add the apples and enough of the remaining water and an equivalent amount of sugar if needed to nearly cover the apples. Cook just until the apples are tender-crisp; do not overcook. Drain the apples and spread in a buttered 9×9-inch baking dish.

Combine the almond paste with the eggs in a food processor and process until smooth, or grate the almond paste and use a hand mixer to combine with the eggs. Spread over the apples.

Bake for 40 minutes or until the top is light brown. Serve warm or cold with whipped cream. You can also prepare this with unpeeled tart red or pink apples for an easy and more colorful dessert.

SERVES 9

An Apple a Day

Crunchy, crisp, sweet, and juicy—Washington apples are undeniably scrumptious. Washington State leads the country in apple production, producing some 2.4 million tons of apples each year. More than half the apples grown in the United States for eating fresh come from the picturesque Washington orchards. In addition to being sold in all fifty states, Washington apples are marketed in more than forty countries. Washington is best known for its handpicked red Delicious, golden Delicious, Gala, Fuji, Granny Smith, and Jonagold varieties.

Reprinted with permission of
The Olympian/Steven Herppich

Lemon Tart with Fresh Blueberries

Juice of 2 lemons, strained
3/4 cup (about) bottled
   lemon juice
1 1/4 cups sugar
4 eggs, beaten
Grated zest of 2 lemons

1/4 cup (1/2 stick) butter,
   chopped
1 partially baked Tart Crust
   (below)
Fresh blueberries
Whipped cream

Preheat the oven to 300 degrees. Combine the fresh lemon juice with enough bottled lemon juice to measure 1 cup. Combine with the sugar in a saucepan and stir to dissolve the sugar. Add the eggs and lemon zest and mix well.

Cook just until thickened, whisking constantly; do not overcook. Whisk in the butter and remove from the heat. Spoon into the Tart Crust.

Bake for 40 minutes or until set. Let cool to room temperature. Chill in the refrigerator. Top with blueberries and whipped cream to serve.

SERVES 6

Tart Crust

1 cup all-purpose flour
1/3 cup confectioners' sugar

1/2 cup (1 stick) butter, chilled
   and chopped

Preheat the oven to 350 degrees. Process the flour and confectioners' sugar in a food processor until mixed. Add the butter gradually, processing constantly until the mixture forms clumps. Remove to a mixing bowl and mix by hand until smooth.

Press the dough into a tart pan sprayed with nonstick cooking spray; trim the edge. Pierce with a fork. Place in the freezer for 15 minutes. Bake for 10 minutes. Let cool to room temperature.

MAKES 1 CRUST

Blackberry Crisp

3 cups fresh or frozen
   blackberries
2 tablespoons all-purpose flour
1 cup granulated sugar
2 tablespoons fresh lemon juice
1/8 teaspoon salt

1 cup rolled oats
3/4 cup all-purpose flour
3/4 cup packed brown sugar
1/2 teaspoon nutmeg
Salt to taste
1/2 cup (1 stick) butter, softened

Preheat the oven to 375 degrees. Combine the blackberries with 2 tablespoons flour, the granulated sugar, lemon juice and 1/8 teaspoon salt in a bowl and mix gently. Spoon into a 9-inch baking dish.

Combine the oats, 3/4 cup flour, the brown sugar, nutmeg and salt to taste in a bowl. Add the butter and mix with your fingers until the mixture is the consistency of crumbs. Sprinkle over the blackberries.

Bake for 50 to 55 minutes or until the topping is brown. Serve at room temperature with vanilla ice cream.

SERVES 6

Baker's Cream

3/4 cup sugar
6 egg yolks
1 tablespoon vanilla extract

3/4 cup heavy cream
3/4 cup half-and-half
Brown sugar

Preheat the oven to 325 degrees. Combine the sugar, egg yolks and vanilla in a large bowl and mix until smooth. Combine the heavy cream and half-and-half in a microwave-safe bowl. Microwave on High for 1 minute. Add to the egg yolk mixture very gradually, mixing constantly.

Pour into four 6- or 8-ounce custard dishes. Place in a 9×13-inch baking pan and add enough hot water to reach halfway up the sides of the custard dishes. Bake for 45 to 55 minutes or until set. Cool in the freezer. Sift brown sugar over the tops and brown under the broiler or with a kitchen torch.

SERVES 4

Cheesecake with Apricot Brandy Sauce

16 ounces cream
cheese, softened
1/3 cup sugar
4 eggs
Juice and grated zest of
1 lemon
1 teaspoon vanilla extract

1 Cheesecake Crust (below)
2 cups sour cream
1/2 cup sugar
1 teaspoon vanilla extract
Apricot Brandy Sauce
(page 163)

Preheat the oven to 375 degrees. Combine the cream cheese, 1/3 cup sugar, the eggs, lemon juice, lemon zest and 1 teaspoon vanilla in a mixing bowl and mix until smooth. Spread over the Cheesecake Crust. Bake for 25 minutes or until set.

Combine the sour cream, 1/2 cup sugar and 1 teaspoon vanilla in a bowl and mix well. Spread over the cheesecake.

Bake for 5 to 7 minutes longer or until set. Spoon Apricot Brandy Sauce over the top to serve.

SERVES 12

Cheesecake Crust

1 3/4 cups graham cracker crumbs
1 tablespoon all-purpose flour
1 tablespoon sugar
1/4 cup (1/2 stick) butter

Combine the graham cracker crumbs, flour and sugar in a bowl. Add the butter and mix with your fingers or a pastry blender. Press firmly over the bottom of a 9-inch springform pan.

MAKES 1 CRUST

Apricot Brandy Sauce

1/2 cup sugar
1/3 cup water
1 pound firm ripe apricots
1 tablespoon lemon juice
Cinnamon to taste
1/3 cup brandy

Bring the sugar and water to a boil in a heavy 10-quart saucepan, stirring to dissolve the sugar completely. Reduce the heat to low. Add the apricots and bring to a boil. Cook until the apricots are very tender, stirring occasionally. Add the lemon juice and cinnamon; cool.

Process the sauce in a food processor or blender for about 1 minute or until smooth. Add the brandy. Serve on cheesecake, ice cream, vanilla yogurt or pound cake, or use to glaze chicken, ham, pork roast, or turkey breast. You may substitute one 16-ounce can apricots for the fresh apricots. Drain, reserving the juice for part of the water.

MAKES 3 CUPS

Strawberry Cream Crunch

1/2 cup (1 stick) butter, softened
1/4 cup packed brown sugar
1 cup all-purpose flour
1/2 cup nuts
1 cup heavy whipping cream
1 teaspoon vanilla extract
2 egg whites, lightly beaten
1 cup granulated sugar
1 tablespoon lemon juice
1 tablespoon vanilla extract
1 (10-ounce) package frozen
    strawberries, sprinkled with
    1 teaspoon sugar

Preheat the oven to 350 degrees. Combine the butter, brown sugar, flour and nuts in a bowl and mix well. Spread on a baking sheet. Bake until light brown, stirring frequently; the mixture will be crumbly. Spread three-fourths of the crumb mixture in a freezer-safe 9×13-inch dish.

Whip the cream with 1 teaspoon vanilla in a bowl. Combine the egg whites with the granulated sugar, lemon juice, 1 tablespoon vanilla and the strawberries in a mixing bowl. Beat for 10 minutes. Fold in the whipped cream. Spread in the prepared dish and top with the remaining crumb mixture. Freeze until firm.

SERVES 12

Lemon Ice

¹/4 cup lemon juice
1 cup (scant) sugar
1 cup heavy whipping cream,
  whipped

1 cup milk
¹/2 teaspoon lemon extract
12 drops of yellow food coloring
  (optional)

Mix the lemon juice and sugar in a bowl. Add the whipped cream, milk, lemon extract and food coloring; mix gently. Spoon into a freezer-safe 8×11-inch pan or ice cube trays without dividers. Freeze for 1 hour. Stir to mix well and freeze until firm. Serve like ice cream.

SERVES 8

Coconut Bread Pudding

8 ounces dry baguette, cut into
  1-inch pieces
¹/4 cup dried apricots, chopped
¹/2 cup shredded coconut
2 cups milk

2 (15-ounce) cans cream
  of coconut
2 tablespoons vanilla extract
¹/2 cup sugar
8 egg yolks

Preheat the oven to 350 degrees. Place the bread in a 4-quart baking dish and top with the apricots and coconut. Combine the milk, cream of coconut, vanilla and half the sugar in a saucepan. Heat just to 140 degrees, stirring to dissolve the sugar completely.

Beat the remaining sugar with the egg yolks in a stand mixer until smooth. Add the milk mixture gradually, mixing until the sugar dissolves. Pour over the layers in the baking dish. Let stand for 15 minutes.

Cover tightly with plastic wrap and then foil. Place in a large roasting pan and add 2 inches water. Bake for 50 minutes. Reduce the oven temperature to 275 degrees and bake for 10 minutes longer. Remove the foil and plastic wrap and let cool to room temperature. Store, covered, in the refrigerator.

SERVES 8

164

Sour Cream Apple Cake

2 cups all-purpose flour
2 cups packed brown sugar
1/2 cup (1 stick) butter, softened
1 cup chopped pecans
1 cup sour cream
1 egg, beaten

1 teaspoon baking soda
2 teaspoons cinnamon
1 teaspoon vanilla extract
1/2 teaspoon salt
2 cups finely chopped
    peeled apples

Preheat the oven to 350 degrees. Combine the flour, brown sugar and butter in a mixing bowl. Mix at low speed until crumbly. Stir in the pecans. Press 2 3/4 cups of the pecan mixture in an ungreased 9×13-inch baking pan.

Add the sour cream, egg, baking soda, cinnamon, vanilla and salt to the remaining pecan mixture and mix well. Stir in the apples. Spoon evenly over the prepared layer.

Bake for 25 to 30 minutes or until a wooden pick inserted into the center comes out clean. Cut into squares and serve warm or cold with whipped cream or ice cream.

SERVES 12

Inspiration

Children cannot vote or advocate for themselves. As caring women, Junior Leagues unite to help pass laws which make a difference in the lives of our children. The Junior Leagues throughout Washington State gather annually during the legislative sessions in Olympia for **Capitol Days**. Members are educated about specific bills and meet with their local representatives. Junior League of Olympia is committed to healthy families by building awareness of ways to prevent child abuse and neglect.

Apple Walnut Cake

4 cups coarsely chopped apples
2 cups sugar
2 cups sifted all-purpose flour
2 teaspoons baking soda
1 1/2 teaspoons cinnamon
1/2 teaspoon nutmeg

1 teaspoon salt
2 eggs
1/2 cup vegetable oil
2 teaspoons vanilla extract
1 cup walnuts, chopped
Apple Cake Sauce (below)

Preheat the oven to 375 degrees. Mix the apples and sugar in a bowl and let stand for several minutes. Sift the flour with the baking soda, cinnamon, nutmeg and salt. Beat the eggs lightly in a bowl; beat in the oil and vanilla. Stir the dry ingredients into the egg mixture alternately with the apples. Stir in the walnuts.

Spoon the batter into a greased and floured 9×13-inch cake pan. Bake for 50 minutes or until the cake tests done. Serve with warm Apple Cake Sauce. You can also serve this with lemon butter frosting or a simple sugar glaze.

SERVES 12

Apple Cake Sauce

1 cup sugar
1/2 cup (1 stick) butter
1/2 cup heavy cream or evaporated milk
2 tablespoons lemon juice
1 teaspoon vanilla extract

Combine the sugar, butter, cream, lemon juice and vanilla in a saucepan and mix well. Bring to a boil over medium-high heat and cook for 3 minutes, stirring frequently. Serve warm over Apple Walnut Cake.

MAKES 2 CUPS

3 cups all-purpose flour
1 tablespoon baking powder
1 tablespoon baking soda
$4^1/2$ teaspoons cinnamon
$1/2$ teaspoon each nutmeg,
    ground cloves and ginger
$1/4$ teaspoon salt
3 cups sugar
6 eggs

$2^1/4$ cups vegetable oil
1 tablespoon vanilla extract
6 cups packed grated carrots
1 cup golden raisins
1 cup shredded coconut
1 cup walnuts, broken into
    medium-size pieces
Cream Cheese Frosting (below)
$3/4$ cup finely chopped walnuts

Preheat the oven to 350 degrees. Butter three 9-inch cake pans and line the bottoms with circles of waxed paper. Butter and flour the waxed paper, shaking out any excess flour.

Sift the flour, baking powder, baking soda, cinnamon, nutmeg, cloves, ginger and salt together. Combine the sugar and eggs in a mixing bowl and beat until thickened. Beat in the oil gradually. Stir in the flour mixture. Add the vanilla. Fold in the carrots, raisins, coconut and 1 cup walnuts.

Spread equal amounts of the batter in the prepared cake pans. Bake for 35 to 40 minutes or until the tops spring back when lightly touched. Remove to a wire rack to cool. Spread Cream Cheese Frosting between the layers and over the top and side of the cake. Press 3/4 cup walnuts over the side of the cake. Chill for 8 hours or longer before serving.

SERVES 12

Cream Cheese Frosting

16 ounces cream cheese, slightly softened
4 cups confectioners' sugar, sifted

Beat the cream cheese in a mixing bowl until smooth. Add the confectioners' sugar and beat at a high speed until light and fluffy.

FROSTS ONE 3-LAYER CAKE

Chocolate Mocha Layer Cake

2 1/2 cups cake flour, sifted
1 tablespoon baking powder
1/2 teaspoon salt
3/4 cup (1 1/2 sticks)
   butter, softened
1 1/4 cups sugar
5 egg yolks

2 teaspoons vanilla extract
1 1/4 cups milk
1/4 cup walnuts, finely chopped
Mocha Buttercream Frosting
   (below)
Chocolate Glaze (page 169)

Preheat the oven to 350 degrees. Sift the flour with the baking powder and salt. Beat the butter, sugar, egg yolks and vanilla in a large mixing bowl at high speed for 3 minutes. Add the flour mixture alternately with the milk, stirring by hand until smooth after each addition. Stir in the walnuts. Spoon into two greased and floured 9-inch cake pans. Bake for 30 minutes. Cool in the pans on wire racks for 10 minutes; loosen the edges and remove to the wire rack to cool completely. Split each layer into halves horizontally to make four layers.

Spread Mocha Buttercream Frosting between the layers and over the top and side of the cake. Drizzle with Chocolate Glaze. Garnish with walnut halves.

SERVES 12

168

Mocha Buttercream Frosting

3 ounces semisweet chocolate
1/2 cup (1 stick) butter
2 teaspoons instant espresso
   coffee granules

1/3 cup warm water
1 (1-pound) package
   confectioners' sugar

Melt the chocolate and butter in a saucepan over low heat. Dissolve the coffee granules in the water in a cup. Blend with the confectioners' sugar in a large bowl. Add the chocolate mixture and place over a bowl of ice water. Beat with a wooden spoon until thick.

FROSTS 1 LAYER CAKE

Chocolate Glaze

2 ounces semisweet chocolate
2 tablespoons butter
1 teaspoon vanilla extract
1 tablespoon confectioners' sugar

Combine the chocolate, butter and vanilla in a microwave-safe bowl and microwave until melted. Stir in the confectioners' sugar.

MAKES 1/4 CUP

Lemon Cake with Sour Cream

2 cups all-purpose flour
2 teaspoons baking powder
1 teaspoon salt
1 cup (2 sticks) butter, softened
2 cups granulated sugar
3 eggs
Grated zest of 1 large lemon
1 cup sour cream
1/4 cup (1/2 stick) butter, melted
2 tablespoons fresh lemon juice
2 cups confectioners' sugar, sifted

Preheat the oven to 325 degrees. Sift the flour with the baking powder and salt. Combine 1 cup butter and the granulated sugar in a mixing bowl and beat at high speed with a hand mixer for 5 minutes or until light and fluffy. Beat in the eggs one at a time, scraping down the side of the bowl frequently. Mix in the lemon zest. Add the flour mixture one-third at a time, alternating with the sour cream and mixing until smooth after each addition.

Spoon the batter into a buttered and floured 10-inch bundt pan. Bake for 55 to 65 minutes or until a cake tester or wooden pick inserted near the center comes out clean. Cool in the pan for 10 minutes. Combine 1/4 cup butter, the lemon juice and confectioners' sugar in a bowl and mix until smooth. Invert the cake onto a platter and drizzle evenly with the glaze.

SERVES 12 TO 15

Pumpkin Pistachio Pear Cake

2 cups all-purpose flour
2 teaspoons baking powder
1 teaspoon baking soda
2 teaspoons cinnamon
1/2 teaspoon salt
4 eggs
2 cups sugar

1 cup canola oil
1 (15-ounce) can pumpkin
1 teaspoon vanilla extract
1/2 cup pistachios
1/2 cup chopped pear
Creamy Frosting (below)

Preheat the oven to 350 degrees. Sift the flour with the baking powder, baking soda, cinnamon and salt. Beat the eggs lightly in a bowl. Add the sugar, canola oil, pumpkin and vanilla and beat until smooth. Add the flour mixture and mix until smooth. Fold in the pistachios and pear.

Spoon the batter into a greased and floured bundt pan or tube pan. Bake for 1 hour or until the cake tests done with a wooden pick. Cool in the pan on a wire rack. Invert the cake onto a cake plate and spread with Creamy Frosting. Garnish with additional chopped pistachios.

SERVES 12

Creamy Frosting

6 tablespoons butter, softened
8 ounces cream cheese,
    softened
1 tablespoon milk

1 teaspoon vanilla extract
1 (1-pound) package
    confectioners' sugar

Combine the butter, cream cheese, milk and vanilla in a mixing bowl and mix well. Add the confectioners' sugar and beat until smooth.

FROSTS 1 CAKE

Sticky Toffee Cake

1¹/2 cups chopped dates
1¹/2 cups water
1¹/2 teaspoons baking soda
1¹/4 cups packed light
    brown sugar
6 tablespoons unsalted
    butter, softened

3 eggs
1¹/2 teaspoons vanilla extract
1 teaspoon ginger
¹/4 teaspoon baking powder
2 cups all-purpose flour
Toffee Sauce (below)

Preheat the oven to 350 degrees. Combine the dates and water in a small saucepan and bring to a boil. Reduce the heat and simmer for 5 minutes. Remove from the heat and stir in the baking soda.

Cream the brown sugar and butter at high speed in a large mixing bowl until light and fluffy. Beat in the eggs one at a time. Add the vanilla, ginger and baking powder and mix well. Stir in the flour and the date mixture gradually.

Spoon into a buttered 9×12-inch baking pan or 10-inch springform pan. Bake for 45 to 60 minutes or until a knife inserted into the center comes out moist but clean. Poke holes in the cake and drizzle a small amount of Toffee Sauce over the top. Cut into pieces and serve the remaining Toffee Sauce hot or cold with the cake. Garnish with fresh greenery and whipped cream to serve during the holidays.

SERVES 12 TO 15

Toffee Sauce

¹/4 cup (¹/2 stick) unsalted
    butter, melted
1 cup packed brown sugar

2/3 cup light corn syrup
¹/8 teaspoon salt
2/3 cup heavy whipping cream

Combine the butter, brown sugar, corn syrup and salt in a heavy saucepan. Bring to a boil over medium heat and stir to mix well. Boil for 3 minutes or until thickened to the consistency of corn syrup; do not stir. Let cool slightly and then stir in the cream.

MAKES 2¹/2 CUPS

Cherry Almond Crumb Pie

3 (14-ounce) cans sour
   cherries for pie
3/4 cup granulated sugar
3 tablespoons cornstarch
1/4 teaspoon almond extract
1/4 teaspoon red food coloring

1 unbaked (9-inch) pie shell
2/3 cup all-purpose flour
1/3 cup packed brown sugar
1/3 cup butter
1/2 cup slivered almonds

Preheat the oven to 400 degrees. Drain the cherries, reserving one cup of the juice. Mix the granulated sugar and cornstarch in a saucepan and stir in the reserved cherry juice. Cook over medium heat until thickened, stirring constantly. Remove from the heat and stir in the cherries, almond extract and food coloring. Spoon into the pie shell.

Combine the flour with the brown sugar and butter in a bowl and mix with a pastry blender until the consistency of coarse cornmeal. Mix in the almonds. Sprinkle over the pie.

Bake for 30 to 40 minutes or until the filling is bubbly and the crust is golden brown. Cut into wedges to serve.

SERVES 6 TO 8

Blackberry Pie

2 cups all-purpose flour, sifted
3 tablespoons confectioners'
   sugar
1/4 teaspoon salt
2/3 cup butter-flavor shortening
1 tablespoon butter

1/2 cup whipping cream
1 cup granulated sugar
3 tablespoons cornstarch
1/2 cup whipping cream
4 cups fresh Northwest
   blackberries

Sift the flour, confectioners' sugar and salt into a bowl. Cut in the shortening and butter with a pastry blender or two knives, mixing to the consistency of large grains of sand. Add 1/2 cup whipping cream and mix with a fork. Shape the dough into a ball and divide into two equal portions. Flatten each portion into a disk and wrap in plastic wrap. Chill for 15 minutes.

Combine the granulated sugar, cornstarch and 1/2 cup whipping cream in a bowl and mix to form a smooth paste. Fold in the blackberries.

Preheat the oven to 375 degrees. Roll each portion of dough into a circle on a lightly floured surface, rolling between sheets of plastic wrap if necessary. Fit one dough circle into a pie plate.

Spoon the blackberry mixture into the prepared pie plate and top with the remaining dough circle. Trim the edge and cut vents in the top. Cover the edge with foil or a pie crust protector. Bake for 35 to 45 minutes or until the crust is golden brown. Let cool before cutting into wedges to serve.

To use frozen blackberries, defrost in a colander to remove excess liquid and reduce the amount of whipping cream in the filling to 1/3 cup.

SERVES 6 TO 8

A Picking We Will Go

On any warm day in late summer, you will find people, young and old, along the sides of rural Northwest roads vigorously picking wild blackberries from prickly bushes. These dark purple berries are sweet, tart, and colorful, and can be used in desserts, sprinkled on salads, or popped in your mouth straight from the bush.

Mocha Gelato Pie

1/4 cup chocolate sauce
1 Pecan Crust (below)
1 1/2 pints good-quality
    chocolate gelato, softened

1/4 cup coffee liqueur
1 1/2 pints good-quality vanilla
    gelato or coffee gelato,
    softened
1/4 cup chocolate sauce

Drizzle 1/4 cup chocolate sauce over the Pecan Crust. Spread the chocolate gelato over the crust and freeze for several hours. Blend the liqueur with the vanilla gelato in a bowl. Spread over the frozen layer and freeze until serving time.

Let the pie stand at room temperature for 15 minutes. Drizzle 1/4 cup chocolate sauce in a decorative pattern over the top. Cut into wedges to serve.

SERVES 6 TO 8

Pecan Crust

1 1/2 cups finely chopped pecans
1/4 cup sugar
1 egg white, lightly beaten

Preheat the oven to 350 degrees. Mix the pecans, sugar and egg white in a bowl. Press into a 9-inch pie pan. Bake for 10 minutes or until light brown. Let cool to room temperature.

MAKES 1 CRUST

Candy Bar Fudge

1/2 cup (1 stick) butter
   or margarine
1/3 cup baking cocoa
1/4 cup packed brown sugar
1/4 cup milk
31/2 cups confectioners' sugar
1 teaspoon vanilla extract

30 caramel candies
1 tablespoon water
2 cups salted peanuts
1/2 cup (3 ounces) semisweet
   chocolate chips
1/2 cup (3 ounces) milk
   chocolate chips

Combine the first four ingtredients in a microwave-safe bowl. Microwave on High for 3 minutes or until boiling. Stir in the confectioners' sugar and vanilla. Press into a greased 8×8-inch pan.

Combine the caramel candies and water in a microwave-safe bowl. Microwave on High for 2 minutes or until the caramels melt. Stir in the peanuts. Spread over the chocolate layer. Combine the chocolate chips in a microwave-safe bowl. Microwave on High for 1 minute or until melted. Spread over the caramel layer. Chill until firm. Cut into squares.

MAKES 36

Pumpkin Fudge

3 cups sugar
1 cup milk
3 tablespoons corn syrup
1/2 cup mashed cooked fresh or
   canned pumpkin

1/4 teaspoon salt
1/2 cup (1 stick) butter
1/2 cup nuts, chopped (optional)
11/2 teaspoons vanilla extract
1 teaspoon pumpkin pie spice

Bring the sugar, milk, corn syrup, pumpkin and salt to a boil in a 3-quart saucepan over high heat, stirring constantly. Reduce the heat to medium and boil to 232 degrees on a candy thermometer, soft-ball stage; do not stir. Remove from the heat and stir in the butter, nuts, vanilla and pumpkin pie spice. Let cool to 110 degrees on a candy thermometer, lukewarm. Beat until the mixture is very thick and loses some of its gloss. Pour immediately into a greased 8×8-inch pan. Let stand until firm. Cut into squares.

MAKES 36

Chocolate Crunch Brownies

1 cup (2 sticks) butter or
  margarine, softened
2 cups sugar
4 eggs
1 cup all-purpose flour
6 tablespoons baking cocoa
1/2 teaspoon salt

2 teaspoons vanilla extract
1 (7-ounce) jar
  marshmallow creme
2 cups (12 ounces) semisweet
  chocolate chips
1 cup peanut butter
3 cups crisp rice cereal

Preheat the oven to 350 degrees. Cream the butter and sugar in a large mixing bowl until light and fluffy. Beat in the eggs. Stir in the flour, baking cocoa, salt and vanilla. Spread in a greased 9×13-inch baking pan. Bake for 20 to 25 minutes or until the brownies test done. Let cool to room temperature. Spread with the marshmallow creme.

Combine the chocolate chips and peanut butter in a large saucepan. Heat over low heat until melted, stirring constantly. Remove from the heat and stir in the cereal. Spread over the marshmallow layer. Chill in the refrigerator. Cut into squares to serve. Store any leftovers in the refrigerator.

MAKES 36

1/2 cup (1 stick) butter, melted
2 cups sugar
11/2 cups all-purpose flour
1/2 cup baking cocoa
4 eggs

2 teaspoons vanilla extract
1/4 teaspoon salt
1/2 cup nuts
Brownie Frosting (below)

Fabulous Brownies

Preheat the oven to 350 degrees. Combine the butter, sugar, flour, baking cocoa, eggs, vanilla and salt in a mixing bowl and mix well. Stir in the nuts.

Spoon the batter into a 9×13-inch baking pan. Bake for 25 minutes. Let cool to room temperature. Spread Brownie Frosting over the brownies. Cut into squares.

MAKES 36

3 tablespoons butter
3 tablespoons baking cocoa
1/3 cup packed brown sugar
1/4 cup milk

Salt to taste
1 cup confectioners' sugar
1 teaspoon vanilla extract

Brownie Frosting

Combine the butter, baking cocoa, brown sugar, milk and salt in a saucepan. Cook over low heat until the butter melts, stirring to blend well. Remove from the heat and let cool slightly. Add the confectioners' sugar and vanilla and mix well.

FROSTS 1 (9×13-INCH) PAN
OF BROWNIES

Maple Chocolate Bars

1 1/2 cups all-purpose flour
2/3 cup sugar
1/2 teaspoon salt
3/4 cup (1 1/2 sticks) butter or
    margarine, chilled
1 egg

1 cup (6 ounces) semisweet
    chocolate chips
1 (14-ounce) can sweetened
    condensed milk
1 egg
2 cups walnuts, chopped
1 1/2 teaspoons maple flavoring

Preheat the oven to 350 degrees. Mix the flour, sugar and salt in a bowl. Cut in the butter until the consistency of coarse crumbs. Add one egg and mix well. Spread in a 9×13-inch baking pan. Bake for 25 minutes. Maintain the oven temperature. Sprinkle with the chocolate chips.

Combine the condensed milk, one egg, the walnuts and maple flavoring in a bowl; mix well. Spread over the chocolate chip layer. Bake for 30 minutes longer. Let cool to room temperature and then cut into squares.

MAKES 24

2 (8-ounce) packages
   chopped dates
1 cup packed brown sugar
1 cup water
1 cup plus 2 tablespoons
   butter

1¹/2 cups packed brown sugar
1¹/2 cups all-purpose flour
1¹/2 teaspoons baking soda
3 cups thick-cut oats

Preheat the oven to 375 degrees. Combine the dates, 1 cup brown sugar and the water in a saucepan. Cook over medium heat for 5 to 7 minutes or until thickened and bubbly, stirring constantly and mashing with a potato masher. Let cool to room temperature.

Cream the butter and 1¹/2 cups brown sugar in a mixing bowl until light and fluffy. Add the flour, baking soda and oats. Mix until crumbly. Press half over the bottom of a greased 9×13-inch baking pan.

Spread the cooled date mixture in the prepared pan and sprinkle the remaining crumb mixture over the top. Bake for 25 minutes. Let cool to room temperature and then cut into bars. Serve in paper pastry cups.

MAKES 24

2 cups rolled oats
1 cup all-purpose flour

¹/2 cup sugar
1 cup (2 sticks) butter, softened

Preheat the oven to 350 degrees. Combine the oats, flour, sugar and butter in a bowl and mix to form a dough. Shape into walnut-size balls. Place on a baking sheet and press with a fork. Bake for 10 minutes.

MAKES 36

Mocha Truffle Cookies

2 cups all-purpose flour
1/3 cup unsweetened baking cocoa (not Dutch process)
1/2 teaspoon baking powder
1/4 teaspoon salt
1/2 cup (1 stick) butter
1/2 cup (3 ounces) semisweet chocolate chips
3/4 cup granulated sugar
3/4 cup packed brown sugar
1 tablespoon instant coffee granules or espresso granules
2 eggs, beaten
2 teaspoons vanilla extract
1 cup (6 ounces) semisweet chocolate chips

Preheat the oven to 350 degrees. Mix the flour with the baking cocoa, baking powder and salt in a medium bowl.

Melt the butter with 1/2 cup chocolate chips in a medium saucepan over medium heat. Stir in the granulated sugar, brown sugar and coffee granules. Remove from the heat. Add the eggs and vanilla and mix well. Stir in the flour mixture and 1 cup chocolate chips.

Spoon by heaping tablespoonfuls onto a greased cookie sheet. Bake for just 10 minutes. Let cool on the cookie sheet for 1 minute and then remove to a wire rack to cool. Store in an airtight container.

MAKES 36

Northwest Inspirations Committee

Thank you to all Junior League of Olympia members, family, and friends
for making this cookbook possible—what an inspiration!

2006–07
CHAIR
Katie Hurley

COMMITTEE
Cynthia Alexander
Shirley Battan
Christy Berschauer
Sue Cook
Samantha Dille
Kathy Garrett
Ruthann Goularte
Michelle Green
Lorraine Hamilton
Judy Henderson
Liz Kapust
Shana Konschuh
Kathy McDowell
Eugenia Michel
Cory Plantenberg
Alicia Quebedeaux
Teri Ryan
Kaye Smith
Laura Theis
Gail Yamane

2007–08
CHAIR
Michelle Green

COMMITTEE
Shirley Battan
Christy Berschauer
Connie Bloom
Samantha Dille
Ruthann Goularte
Lorraine Hamilton
Judy Henderson
Katie Hurley
Liz Kapust
Kathy McDowell
Cory Plantenberg
Jennifer Plichta
Alicia Quebedeaux
Teri Ryan
Vicki Smith
Laura Theis
Jamie Tosland
Gail Yamane

SPONSORSHIPS
Katie Hurley
Alicia Quebedeaux
Vicki Smith
Jamie Tosland

ART/DESIGN
Ruthann Goularte
Lorraine Hamilton
Alicia Quebedeaux

RECIPES
Shirley Battan
Christy Berschauer
Samantha Dille
Judy Henderson
Katie Hurley
Cory Plantenberg
Jennifer Plichta
Teri Ryan
Gail Yamane

NONRECIPE
TEXT/EDITING:
Shirley Battan
Gail Gosney
Michelle Green
Lisa Herrick
Katie Hurley
Linda Kleingartner
Kathy McDowell
Tanya Murray
Cory Plantenberg
Teri Ryan
Diana Stroble
Jamie Tosland

181

JUNIOR LEAGUE OF OLYMPIA
Women building better communities

Live Your Potential, Make a Difference, Feel the Impact.

Sponsors

The continuing support of our sponsors allows the Junior League of Olympia to give back to the community. Thank you.

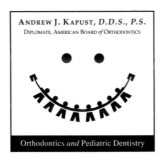

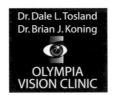

Chef de Cuisine

Capitol City Honda/Kelly Levesque

Sous Chef

Heritage Bank
Andrew J. Kapust, DDS, PS
Olympia Vision Clinic
Austin Rob Smith, DDS

Platinum Whisk

Berschauer Construction, Inc.
Drees/Ruthann Goularte
Tom and Lisa Herrick
John and Katie Hurley
Naturipe Farms

Golden Fork

Paul Battan, Attorney at Law
Dennis and Connie Bloom
Joseph Y. de Jesus, DDS, PS
Rick and Ellen Middleton
Dr. Richard and Laurel Seaman
Anonymous

Silver Spoon

Creatively Organized
Commercial Design
Kathy Garrett
Phil and Michelle Green
Andy and Liz Kapust
Penny Hill Keirsey
Chris and Leslie Merchant
Rick and Christy Peters
Laura Roloff
Doug and Penny Sampson
Vicki Smith
Solid Business Solutions
Peter and Diana Stroble
Bruce and Laura Theis

Bronze Knife

ABC Pediatrics
Joe and Mary de Jesus
Bonnie Finn
David and Jennifer Forster
Wendy Gauksheim
Jacki and Bill Gavin
Jim and Janelle Guthrie
Jane Lane
Chris and Kelly Levesque
Rob and Toni-Ann Little
Bev McKillip
Jacque and Erin Menard
Mel and Jan Murray
Donald G. Sampson, DDS
Jane Sands
Laurie Sorensen and
Carroll Bryan
Eric and Sherrie Smith
William Brown/State Farm
Stormans Inc—
Bayview School of Cooking
Sunset Air
Mia Sweeney
Wendy Tanner
Mary Ann Vetter
Vetter Dental Group
Joanna West
Wine Loft

Acknowledgments

The Junior League of Olympia acknowledges and thanks all of its members, family, and friends for contributing to the success of this cookbook—we are truly grateful for your support and inspiration.

Barbara Ackerman
Dennis and Carol Adams
Christine Alexander
Bonnie Anderson
Shannon Austin
Patty Balestra
Lori Bame
Shirley Battan
Susan Beatty
Beth Berschauer
Christy Berschauer
Cindy Brazas
Linnea Bremner
Briney Sea
Gayle Burditt
Jeff Busch
Stephanie Busch
Café Luna
Louise Cartter
Kathy Casey
Erin Cavin
Amelia Cobb
Susan Cook
Teresa Covington
Gwen Davis
Mary de Jesus
Aileen Denton
Norma Detlefsen
Shelby Dickson
Samantha Dille
Peggy Doebel
Kern Dolby
John Edwards
Falls Terrace Restaurant

Jennifer Forster
Katie Frank
Kyle Fulwiler
Kathy Garrett
Gail Gosney
Ruthann Goularte
Karen Graham
Anelle Granger
Doug Green
Ginny Green
Michelle Green
Janelle Guthrie
Melissa Haberman
Pranee Khruasanit Halvorsen
Lorraine Hamilton
Michelle Hamilton
Mollie Hammar
Kay Harrison
Vickie Hayes
Helsing Junction Farm
Judy Henderson
Herban Feast
Laura Herman
Lisa Herrick
Laurie Hulston
Tracey Hunter
Katie Hurley
Dusty Huxford
Kathryn Adams Johnson
Susan Johnson
Lisa Jolly
Liz Kapust
Linda Kaufmann
Penny Keirsey

Linda Kleingartner
Shana Konschuh
Valerie Lamb
Kelly Levesque
Toni-Ann Little
Margo Litwin
Lynn Lloyd
Brita Long
Susan Manthou
Jennifer Matheson
Kristin McCarthy
Marta McClure
Colette McCully
Kathy McDowell
Elizabeth McHugh
Marianne McIntosh
Debbie Meece
Erin Menard
Leslie Merchant
Ellen Middleton
John Miller
Vivian Miller
Christina Miller-Herigstad
Mark Mobley
Doreen Molaniro
Deborah Montelaro
Talitha Mossberger
Tanya Murray
Debbie Neujahr
Linda Newsome
Barbara Nickum
Susan Norton
Donna Overstreet
Sue Overton
Wendy Owens
Stefani Parsons
Christy Peters
Cory Plantenberg

Tom Plantenberg
Jennifer Plichta
Alicia Quebedeaux
Alison Raymond
Cheryl Reeser
Geri Rein
Tammy Rosser
Teri Ryan
Jane Sands
Carolyn Schaut
Laurel Seaman
Carolee Sharp
Megan Short
Mindy Sloaf
Sherrie Smith
Vicki Smith
Judy Soward
Marie Spealman
Hannah Steinweg
Lisa Stock
Diana Stroble
Linda Strong
Katalin Talaber
Wendy Tanner
Jeff Taylor
Laura Theis
Jamie Tosland
Silje Totland
Sally Warjone
Vanessa Wasman
Marcia Waugh
Dixie Webster
Diane Weeden
Joanna West
Mary Jo Wright
Gail Yamane
K. C. Zambrana

Recipe Index

189

Photograph Index

NORTHWEST
Inspirations
FLAVORS OF SOUTH PUGET SOUND

To order additional copies of *Northwest Inspirations* or for
more information, please contact:

Junior League of Olympia
108 State Avenue NW
Olympia, Washington 98501

Telephone: 360-357-6024
E-mail: info@jlolympia.org
Web site: www.jlolympia.org